Step-by-Step Fermentation: 95 Beginner-Friendly Recipes for Fermenting Foods

Street Snack Oasis Hoga

:

Contents

INTRODUCTION

Welcome to Step-by-Step Fermentation: 95 Beginner-Friendly Recipes for Fermenting Foods! With these recipes and instructions, you'll be able to get started in the fascinating and delicious world of food fermentation. Fermented foods have been a part of the human diet for thousands of years, with evidence of Sauerkraut production from as far back as China in 500 B.C.E. Throughout history, different cultures have been fermenting foods for taste, preservation, nutrition, and even medicinal applications.

Today, fermentation is making a long overdue comeback. More and more people are being encouraged to explore the wide variety of recipes available and create deliciously tangy probiotic-rich meals. From basics like kombucha, sauerkraut, and yogurt to innovative recipes like Kimchi Carrot Fries and Chocolate Chaga Kefir Ice Cream, this cookbook has all the tools you need to get started in fermentation.

You'll learn about the science behind fermentation and the various processes involved, such as salt brining, water-bath canning, and lactic acid fermentation. We'll also go over the tools and ingredients you'll need to start fermenting. Whether you're a traditionalist or looking for something a little creative, you'll be sure to find the perfect recipe.

This cookbook contains 95 recipes and step-by-step instructions for beginners, advanced fermenters, and everyone in between. From staying safe while fermenting, to troubleshooting common problems you'll encounter, to delicious and creative recipes for all kinds of dishes, Step-by-Step Fermentation has everything you need to guarantee delicious and nutritious fermentations every time.

Whether you're just getting started or looking to hone your skills, this cookbook is the perfect guide for finding the recipes and techniques you need to make delicious fermented foods. So roll up your sleeves, grab your pot and apron, and let's get cooking! Finally, we want to thank you for choosing Step-by-Step

Fermentation and wish you the best of luck in creating delicious and nourishing fermented foods.

1. Sauerkraut

Sauerkraut is a traditional German side-dish made of fermented cabbage, enjoyed in many countries, including the US. With just a few Ingredients and time, you can make classic sauerkraut that you'll enjoy for weeks to come.
Serving: 6-8 servings
Preparation Time: 10 minutes
Ready Time: 1-2 days

Ingredients:
- 1 head of green cabbage
- 1 tablespoon of sea salt
- 1 tablespoon of caraway seeds (optional)

Instructions:
1. Discard any outer leaves of the cabbage that are badly bruised or discolored. Cut the cabbage in quarters and remove the tough core.
2. Slice the cabbage as thinly as possible or grate it. Place it in a large bowl and sprinkle the sea salt over the cabbage. Using your hands, mix it together and begin to massage it. The salt will start to pull out some of the cabbage's natural moisture, forming some brine.
3. Place the cabbage in a fermentation vessel. Fill the jar with additional brine just until the cabbage is covered.
4. Seal the jar tightly and place in a cool dark place. Check the jar after 24 hours to ensure that all the cabbage is covered in brine. Adding more brine if needed.
5. Store for 1-2 weeks (for desired tartness).

Nutrition information: Serving size: ½ cup (113g). Calories: 19, Total Fat: 0g, Sodium: 881g, Total Carbohydrate: 5g, Dietary Fiber: 2g, Protein: 1g.

2. Kimchi

Kimchi is a traditional Korean condiment made from fermented cabbage seasoned with garlic, ginger, and chilies. It adds a nice tang and spice to

any dish, and can be used as a side dish or ingredient in various types of cuisine.
Serving: 4
Preparation Time: 10 minutes
Ready Time: 10-14 days

Ingredients:

- 1 head of napa cabbage, cut into small pieces
- 2 tablespoon kosher salt
- 3 cloves of minced garlic
- 1 teaspoon minced ginger
- 2 teaspoon gochugaru (Korean chili pepper flakes)
- 1/2 teaspoon fish sauce or 3 tablespoons anchovy paste
- 1 small carrot, julienned
- 1/2 daikon radish, julienned
- 1/4 cup kimchi juice or water

Instructions:

1. In a large bowl, layer the cabbage and sprinkle with salt. Massage the cabbage for several minutes until it has softened and released its juices.
2. In a separate bowl, mix together the garlic, ginger, gochugaru, fish sauce or anchovy paste, and kimchi juice or water.
3. Add the carrot and daikon to the cabbage and mix everything together.
4. Pour the kimchi paste over the cabbage mix and fold everything together until the paste is evenly distributed.
5. Transfer the kimchi to an airtight container or jar.
6. Let the kimchi ferment at room temperature for 10-14 days. During this time, you will need to burp the container each day to release any excess gas.
7. Once the kimchi is ready, move it to the refrigerator. Your kimchi should keep for several months in the refrigerator.

Nutrition information: Serving size: 1/4 cup, Calories: 28, Total Fat: 0 g, Cholesterol: 0 mg, Sodium: 638 mg, Total Carbohydrate: 6 g, Dietary Fiber: 2 g, Sugars: 3 g, Protein: 1 g

3. Fermented pickles

Make the most delicious fermented pickles in your own home with this simple and easy recipe. Enjoy the freshness and tangy flavor of this delicious condiment, with its hassle-free preparation, and without sacrificing any of its beneficial health properties.
Serving: 6-8 servings
Preparation time: 10 Minutes
Ready Time: 4-5 days

Ingredients:
- 2 tablespoons of sea salt
- 2 cups of filtered water
- 5-6 cucumbers, washed and cut into slices
- 2 cloves of garlic
- 1 teaspoon of dill
- 1 teaspoon of mustard seeds
- 2 tablespoons of whey, or 1 probiotic capsule

Instructions:
1. In a medium bowl, mix the sea salt and water until the salt has dissolved completely.
2. Place the cucumber slices in the saltwater and let it sit for 1 hour.
3. After 1 hour, rinse the cucumbers and place them in a different bowl.
4. Add the garlic, dill, mustard seeds, and whey or probiotic capsule and mix it all together.
5. Put the mixture into a quart-sized jar and fill it with filtered water until it is about ¾ full.
6. Place a lid on the jar, and let it sit at room temperature for 4-5 days.
7. After 4-5 days, you will have homemade fermented pickles.

Nutrition information: Fermented pickles are a great source of probiotics, which are live microorganisms that are beneficial to the body. They are also a great source of vitamin C, which is needed for wound healing, as well as vitamins A, B, C, and E. Plus, fermented pickles contain potassium and manganese for overall health.

4. Yogurt

Yogurt is a creamy and delicious dairy product made by fermenting milk with bacteria. It is rich in protein, calcium, and essential vitamins and minerals and its health benefits make it a popular food around the world.
Serving: 4-6 servings
Preparation time: 10 minutes
Ready time: 6-10 hours

Ingredients:
• 4 cups whole milk
• 4 tablespoons plain yogurt as the starter

Instructions:
1. Heat the milk to 185°F in a heavy-bottomed saucepan. Stir frequently with a wooden spoon to make sure the milk doesn't stick and burn.
2. Turn off the heat and cool to 110°F, stirring occasionally.
3. Once the milk is cooled, add the plain yogurt to the milk and stir well.
4. Cover the saucepan with a lid or plastic wrap and leave it in a warm place to ferment for 6-10 hours.
5. Once the yogurt is thick and creamy, remove from the heat and cool.
6. Store the yogurt in the refrigerator for up to 5 days.

Nutrition information (per 4 ounces): 137 calories, 7 grams fat, 10 grams protein, 8 grams carbohydrate, 0 grams fiber, 75 milligrams calcium, and 67 milligrams sodium

5. Kombucha

Kombucha is a fermented tea beverage that is believed to have originated in China more than 2,000 years ago. It is made with a variety of ingredients, including tea, sugar, starter culture, and herbs. It is beneficial to overall health and also promotes gut health, detoxifying the body, and boosting immunity.
Serving: Serves 4
Preparation Time: 10 minutes
Ready Time: 10-14 days

Ingredients:
• 4 cups of filtered water

• 2 tablespoons of loose-leaf tea (black, green, white, or oolong)
• ¼ cup of sugar
• 2 tablespoons of kombucha starter or store-bought kombucha
• Optional: fresh or dried herbs, fruits, and spices of your choice, such as ginger, basil, lemon, and mint

Instructions:
1. Bring 4 cups of filtered water to a boil in a medium pot.
2. Add the loose-leaf tea to the boiling water and let steep for 5 minutes.
3. Remove the pot from the heat and stir in the sugar until it's fully dissolved.
4. Let the tea mixture cool until it reaches room temperature.
5. Add the kombucha starter or the store-bought kombucha and stir gently.
6. Pour the mixture into a half-gallon glass jar.
7. Add any herbs, fruits, or spices of your choice.
8. Cover the jar with a cheesecloth or paper towel and secure with a rubber band.
9. Place the jar in a warm, dry place (70-80°F is ideal) and let it sit for 10-14 days, or until the kombucha is slightly effervescent.
10. Once ready, can strain the kombucha and transfer it to bottles. Keep it refrigerated for up to two weeks.

Nutrition information: Not Available

6. Sourdough bread

Sourdough bread is a type of bread popular for its crisp crust and chewy texture. It is made using a dough starter, which is a combination of flour and water that ferments over several days. The bread is slow-baked over a long period for maximum flavor.
Serving: Makes 1 loaf of bread.
Preparation Time: 4-7 days
Ready Time: 2 hours

Ingredients:
- 2 cups of active sourdough starter
- 2 1/2 cups of all-purpose flour

- 1 teaspoon of active dry yeast
- 2 teaspoons of salt
- 1 cup of warm water

Instructions:

1. In a large bowl, mix together the sourdough starter and the warm water.
2. Add in the yeast, all-purpose flour, and salt, and mix until a sticky dough forms.
3. Cover and let the dough rest for two hours.
4. Preheat the oven to 400°F.
5. Shape the dough into a ball and place it on a greased baking sheet.
6. Bake for 30-40 minutes or until the bread is golden brown and sounds hollow when tapped.
7. Allow the bread to cool completely before slicing.

Nutrition information: Calories per serving: 166; Fat: 0.4g; Cholesterol: 0mg; Sodium: 376mg; Total Carbohydrate: 34.7g; Dietary Fiber: 1.3g; Sugars: 0.3g; Protein: 5.1g.

7. Miso paste

Miso paste is a traditional Japanese seasoning made from fermented soybeans, salt, and a koji starter. Its mellow, umami flavor adds depth and umami complexity to many dishes.
Serving: 4 to 8 servings
Preparation time: 10 minutes
Ready time: 10 minutes

Ingredients:

- 2/3 cup light white miso paste
- 2 tablespoons mirin
- 2 tablespoons sake
- 1 tablespoon agave syrup
- 2 tablespoons olive oil
- 1 teaspoon grated ginger

Instructions:

1. In a small bowl, mix miso paste, mirin, sake, and agave syrup until smooth.
2. Gradually whisk in olive oil until incorporated.
3. Stir in grated ginger until combined.
4. The miso paste is now ready to use in marinades, soups, glazes and more.

Nutrition information:
Calories: 90 kcal, Carbohydrates: 4 g, Protein: 3 g, Fat: 5 g, Saturated Fat: 1 g, Cholesterol: 0 mg, Sodium: 570 mg, Potassium: 105 mg, Fiber: 1 g, Sugar: 3 g, Vitamin A: 1 IU, Vitamin C: 0 mg, Calcium: 3 mg, Iron: 0.3 mg

8. Tempeh

Tempeh is an Indonesian dish made with fermented soybeans that has a nutty, earthy flavor. It's a protein-rich food and is often used as an alternative to meat due to its texture and size.
Serving: Makes 6 servings
Preparation Time: 10 minutes
Ready Time: 30 minutes

Ingredients:
- 2 ½ cups water
- 1½ cups uncooked dried soybeans
- 3 tablespoons tempeh starter (available online or in specialty stores)
- 2 tablespoons canola oil
- 2 tablespoons soy sauce

Instructions:
1. Soak the soybeans in the water for 8-12 hours, then rinse and drain.
2. Preheat the oven to 350 degrees F.
3. Place the soaked soybeans in a pot or Dutch oven, add the tempeh starter, and mix with a wooden spoon until all ingredients are evenly distributed.
4. Bring the mixture to a boil over medium-high heat and cook for 5-7 minutes, stirring constantly.
5. Turn off the heat and let the mixture cool.

6. Coat a baking sheet with oil. Shape the cooled tempeh mixture into desired shapes and place on the prepared baking sheet.
7. Bake for 25-30 minutes or until desired crispiness is achieved.
8. Remove from the oven and let cool. Serve with soy sauce.

Nutrition information: Per serving: 196 calories, 8 g fat, 24 g protein, 7 g carbohydrate, 4 g fiber.

9. Fermented hot sauce

Fermented hot sauce is a spicy sauce with an intense, earthy flavor that can add a burst of flavor to tacos, burgers, and more. This recipe is a fairly easy way of making your own fermented hot sauce from common Ingredients.
Serving: Makes 2 cups
Preparation Time: 15 minutes
Ready Time: 1-6 weeks

Ingredients:
- 2 cups of dried chilis (such as guajillo, ancho, chipotle, or pasilla), stemmed and seeded
- 2 tablespoons of sea salt
- 3 cloves of garlic, peeled
- 2 tablespoons of apple cider vinegar
- 1 tablespoon of honey
- 2 tablespoons of fish sauce

Instructions:
1. Start by soaking the dried chilis in boiling water for 10 minutes. Remove from the water and let cool. Then, combine the chilis, garlic, salt, vinegar, honey and fish sauce in a blender.
2. Blend the mixture until it's a semi-smooth consistency, adding a bit of the soaking water from the dried chilis if the mixture needs more liquid.
3. Pour the mixture into a clean jar and cover it with a cheesecloth, secure it with an elastic band. Place it in a warm, dark place for a minimum of one week and up to 6 weeks.
4. After the fermentation period, add the hot sauce to a blender and pulse until it's a smooth consistency.

5. Taste the sauce and adjust the flavors according to your preference. Heat, saltiness and sweetness can be adjusted by adding more chilis, salt, vinegar, honey or fish sauce.

Nutrition information: Calorie - 10, Protein - 0.2g, Fat - 0.2g, Carbs - 2.3g, Sodium - 360mg

10. Fermented carrots

Fermented carrots are a delicious condiment made through fermentation.They are sweet and tangy and can be added to salads or eaten on their own. Serving: 4-5 Preparation Time: 15 minutes Ready Time: 7-10 days

Ingredients:
- 2 lbs. Carrots - 3 cloves Garlic - 2 tablespoons Sea Salt - 2 tablespoons Honey - 1/4 teaspoon Dried Red Pepper - 3/4 cup Water

Instructions:
1. Scrub the carrots clean and cut into matchsticks.
2. Place the carrots a glass jar along with the garlic, sea salt, honey, and dried red pepper.
3. Pour the water into the jar and stir to combine all the Ingredients.
4. Cover the jar with a cloth and secure with an elastic band.
5. Leave the jar in a cool and dark place for 7-10 days.
6. Once fermented, open the jar and enjoy!

Nutrition information: Serving size: 1/4 cup; Calories: 55; Total Fat: 0g; Sodium: 613mg; Carbohydrates: 13g; Protein: 1g.

11. Fermented beet slices

Fermented beet slices are a great way to give your meals an extra punch of flavor and provide a unique taste to any dish. Despite their strong taste, they are incredibly easy to make and require only a few hours of pre-preparation.
Serving: 6

Preparation time: 5 minutes
Ready time: 24-48 hours

Ingredients:
- 2 large beets, sliced
- 2 tablespoons of sea salt
- 2 tablespoons olive oil
- 2 tablespoons of sugar
- 2 teaspoons of white vinegar
- 2 tablespoons of freshly chopped thyme

Instructions:
1. Slice the beets into one-quarter inch round slices.
2. Place the slices in a medium-sized bowl.
3. Sprinkle the sea salt over the slices.
4. Drizzle the olive oil over the slices.
5. Add the sugar, white vinegar, and thyme.
6. Mix together well.
7. Place the mixture into a mason jar and seal.
8. Place the jar in a cool, dark place and let it ferment for 24-48 hours.

Nutrition information:
Calories: 88
Carbohydrates: 7 g
Protein: 1 g
Fat: 7 g
Sugar: 6 g
Fiber: 1 g

12. Fermented green beans

Fermented green beans, or douchi, are a traditional Chinese condiment made from black beans that have been salted, fermented, and dried. This savory dish is a popular Ingredient in many Asian recipees and a great topping for rice and noodle dishes.
Serving: 2
Preparation time: 10 minutes
Ready time: 1-2 days

Ingredients:
- 1 cup of black beans
- 1/2 cup of salt
- 4 cups of water

Instructions:
1. Start by soaking the black beans in 4 cups of water overnight.
2. The next day, drain the beans and mix them with the salt.
3. Place the beans and salt mixture in a bowl and cover with plastic wrap.
4. Set the bowl in a warm and sunny place for 1-2 days and allow the beans to ferment.
5. Once the beans are fermented, drain them and spread them out on a baking sheet to dry.
6. After 24 hours, the beans should be totally dry and ready for use.

Nutrition information:
Calories: 45
Total fat: 0.4g
Saturated fat: 0.1g
Cholesterol: 0mg
Sodium: 13mg
Total carbohydrates: 7.4g
Protein: 2.4g

13. Fermented cauliflower

Fermented cauliflower is a flavorful dish packed with probiotics and nutrients. It has a crunchy texture and a tangy, slightly sweet flavor.
Serving: 4 servings
Preparation Time: 15 mins
Ready Time: 2-5 days

Ingredients:
- 1 head of cauliflower
- 1/4 cup of salt
- 2 cloves of garlic, minced
- 2 tablespoons of coriander powder

- 1 teaspoon of turmeric powder
- 1 teaspoon of mustard seeds
- 1/4 cup of rice wine vinegar
- 2-3 tablespoons of sugar
- 2-3 tablespoons of water

Instructions:
1. Start by chopping the cauliflower into small florets and place in a large bowl.
2. In a separate bowl, mix together salt, garlic, coriander powder, turmeric, and mustard seeds.
3. Sprinkle the spices mixture over the cauliflower florets and mix until all florets are coated.
4. Pack the spiced cauliflower into a glass jar with a lid.
5. In a separate bowl, mix together vinegar, sugar, and water.
6. Pour the vinegar mixture over the cauliflower to cover them completely.
7. Secure the lid of the jar and place in a warm and dark spot.
8. Let the cauliflower ferment for 2-5 days, depending on desired taste.
9. Serve the fermented cauliflower with desired toppings.

Nutrition information: Amounts per Serving (4 servings); Calories: 36 kcal, Total Fat: 0.1 g, Saturated Fat: 0 g, Trans Fat: 0 g, Cholesterol: 0 mg, Sodium: 2661 mg, Total Carbohydrates: 7.2 g, Dietary Fibre: 2.6 g, Sugars: 0 g, Protein: 1.9 g.

14. Fermented radishes

Fermented radishes is a flavorful side dish that's easy to prepare and offers a unique mix of flavors and textures. This Vietnamese-style dish pairs well with rice dishes as an accompaniment, or it can be eaten as a snack.
Serving: Makes 4 servings.
Preparation Time: 5 minutes.
Ready Time: 24 hours.

Ingredients:
• 1/2 pound radishes, sliced thin

• 1 teaspoon sea salt
• 2 cloves garlic, minced
• 2 tablespoons sugar
• 2 tablespoons fish sauce
• 1/3 cup filtered water

Instructions:
1. Place the sliced radishes into a medium bowl.
2. Sprinkle the salt over the radishes and stir to combine.
3. Let the radishes rest for 5 minutes.
4. Add in the garlic, sugar, fish sauce, and water. Stir to combine.
5. Place the radish mixture into a lidded glass jar. Press down with the back of a spoon to ensure all the Ingredients are submerged in the liquid.
6. Secure the lid and place the jar on a plate or bowl.
7. Refrigerate the jar for 24 hours.
8. Serve the fermented radishes as a side dish.

Nutrition information:
Calories: 54; Fat: 0.3g; Carbs: 11.3g; Fiber: 1.4g; Protein: 1.1g.

15. Fermented cabbage rolls

Fermented Cabbage Rolls is a traditional Eastern European dish that is made from fermented vegetables and cured meats or fish. This dish is not only known for its unique flavor, but also for its many health benefits due to its high content of probiotics.
Serving: 6-8
Preparation Time: 45 minutes
Ready Time: 1 hour

Ingredients:
- 1 large head of cabbage
- 1/2 cup of pickled cucumbers
- 1/2 cup of walnuts
- 3 cloves of garlic
- 2 tablespoons of olive oil
- 1 tablespoon of black pepper
- 1 teaspoon of sea salt

Instructions:
1. Preheat oven to 350°F.
2. Cut the cabbage into thin slices, removing the core.
3. Place in a large bowl, add the cucumbers, walnuts, garlic, olive oil, black pepper and sea salt and mix well.
4. Grease a large baking dish with oil and add the cabbage mixture.
5. Cover the dish with foil and bake for 25 minutes.
6. Remove the foil and bake for an additional 10-15 minutes, until the cabbage is tender.
7. Let cool and enjoy!

Nutrition information (per serving):
Calories: 226, Fat: 17g, Saturated Fat: 2g, Carbohydrates: 11g, Protein: 7g, Fiber: 3g, Cholesterol: 4mg, Sodium: 165mg.

16. Fermented jalapeño peppers

Try fermenting jalapeño peppers for a spicy, sour condiment perfect for tacos, salads, and other dishes. This recipe yields one quart of pickled jalapeños, so adjust the quantity of Ingredients as needed.
Serving: Makes 1 quart
Preparation Time: 30 minutes
Ready Time: 1-2 weeks

Ingredients:
- 6-7 jalapeño peppers
- 3 tablespoons pickling or sea salt
- 2 cloves garlic, peeled
- 2 tablespoons honey
- 2 cups freshly filtered water

Instructions:
1. Rinse the peppers to remove dirt and debris. Slice the peppers in thirds lengthwise and core.
2. Place peppers slices in a sterile Mason jar, alternating with garlic cloves.
3. In a separate bowl, mix salt, honey, and water until salt is dissolved.

4. Add the salt brine to the Mason jar, covering the peppers.
5. Place a fermentation lid or an airlock top on the Mason jar.
6. Place the jar in a cool, dark place for 1-2 weeks to ferment.
7. After the fermentation period, the peppers are ready to eat. Store in the refrigerator for up to 6 months.

Nutrition information: Serving size 1/2 cup. Calories 8, Total Fat 0g, Sodium 611mg, Total Carbohydrate 0g, Protein 0g.

17. Fermented ginger carrots

Fermented ginger carrots are a tangy, tart and unique side dish that pairs well with chicken, fish, pork, salads, and even consorted cheeses. This unexpected and flavorful dish is easy to make and you don't have to wait very long to enjoy the results.
Serving: 4
Preparation time: 10 minutes
Ready time: 2-4 days

Ingredients:
- 2 lbs carrots, peeled and sliced
- ¼ cup fresh ginger, minced
- 1 tsp sea salt
- 2 tsp sugar
- 1 garlic clove, minced
- ¼ cup whey, or juice of 1 lemon
- 2 cups filtered water

Instructions:
1. In a large bowl, combine the carrots, ginger, sea salt, sugar, garlic, whey and filtered water.
2. Use a spoon or your hands to mix everything together.
3. Transfer the mixture to a sterilized glass jar or fermentation vessel. Make sure to leave a few inches of space at the top of the jar.
4. Cover the jar with cheesecloth and secure it with a rubber band.
5. Place the jar in a cool, dark area and allow the mixture to ferment for 2-3 days, or until it tastes tangy and tart. Taste test the mixture every day to determine when it is done.

6. Once it is done, transfer the mixture to mason jars and store them in the refrigerator.

Nutrition information: per serving (1/4 of recipe): 73 calories, 1g fat, 0mg cholesterol, 170mg sodium, 15g carbohydrates, 3g dietary fiber, 8g sugar, 1g protein.

18. Fermented cucumber relish

Fermented cucumber relish is an easy-to-make condiment that adds a unique and flavorful touch to salads, tacos, sandwiches, and more.
Serving: 4
Preparation time: 15 minutes
Ready time: 2-3 days

Ingredients:
• 2 cucumbers, cut into 1/4-inch dice
• 2 tablespoons water
• 2 tablespoons white sugar
• 2 tablespoons white vinegar
• 1 teaspoon salt
• 2 cloves garlic, minced

Instructions:
1. In a medium bowl, mix together cucumbers, water, sugar, vinegar, salt, and garlic.
2. Transfer the mixture to a glass quart jar, making sure to leave at least an inch of headspace at the top of the jar.
3. Cover the jar with a lid and store in a cool, dark place for 2-3 days while it ferments.
4. Once the relish has fermented to your desired level of tartness, place the lid on the jar tightly and store in the refrigerator for up to 1 month.

Nutrition information (per serving):Calories 26; Total Fat 0g; Saturated Fat 0g; Cholesterol 0mg; Sodium 333mg; Total Carbohydrate 6g; Dietary Fiber 0g; Protein 0g.

19. Fermented garlic cloves

Fermented garlic cloves are a delicious and savory condiment that adds a depth of flavor to any meal or snack. The fermentation process brings out the best flavors of garlic and adds a slightly sour zing to your plate.
Serving: 2-3
Preparation time: 10 minutes
Ready time: 10 days

Ingredients:
- 2-3 cloves of garlic, peeled and finely chopped
- 2-3 teaspoons of sea salt
- 2-3 tablespoons of olive oil
- 2-3 tablespoons of freshly squeezed lemon juice

Instructions:
1. Peel and finely chop the garlic cloves.
2. Place garlic cloves in a mason jar or similar container and add salt, olive oil, and lemon juice.
3. Stir thoroughly until the salt and oil are evenly distributed.
4. Place lid on jar and leave out at room temperature for 10 days.
5. Check periodically and stir gently.
6. Once the garlic cloves are fermented to a desired taste, place in the refrigerator.

Nutrition information: Fermented garlic cloves are a rich source of vitamins and minerals, including Vitamin C, magnesium, potassium, and selenium. They are also a good source of dietary fiber.

20. Fermented onion slices

Fermented onion slices bring a unique flavor to a variety of dishes. The fermentation process not only gives the onions a tangy flavor, but it also makes them a healthy probiotic-rich snack.
Serving – 2-3 people
Preparation Time – 15 minutes
Ready Time – 24-36 hours

Ingredients:
•2 cups of thinly sliced white or yellow onion
•2 tablespoons of coarse salt
•2 tablespoons of apple cider vinegar
•1 tablespoon of honey
•2 tablespoons of spring water

Instructions:
1. Slice the onions thinly into rings and place them in a clean bowl.
2. Sprinkle the coarse salt over the onions. Allow the salt to rest on top of the onions for 10 minutes.
3. In a separate bowl, mix together the apple cider vinegar, honey, and water until combined.
4. Pour the vinegar mixture over the onions and stir until evenly mixed.
5. Place the onions in a clean mason jar or storage container. Fill the jar or container with the vinegar juice, leaving about one inch of space at the top.
6. Cover the jar or container with a cheesecloth and store at room temperature in a dark, cool place for 24-36 hours. Check the onions daily to ensure the juice is covering the onions.
7. Once the fermentation period is complete, store the onions in the fridge.

Nutrition information –
Serving size: 1 cup
Calories: 52
Fat: 0.1 g
Carbohydrates: 12.3 g
Protein: 1.2 g
Fiber: 1.7 g
Sodium: 1290.2 mg

21. Fermented bell peppers

Fermented bell peppers is a mouthwateringly delicious side dish made with bell peppers, garlic, and spices. The added fermentation process further enhances the flavor of the peppers with a tangy and salty kick.

Serving: Makes 4-6 Servings
Preparation Time: 10 Minutes
Ready Time: 4 Days

Ingredients:

- 3-4 red bell peppers, capsicum or sweet peppers
- 2 cloves of garlic, finely minced
- 1 teaspoon of salt
- 1 tablespoon of extra-virgin olive oil
- 1/2 teaspoon of sugar
- 1/4 teaspoon of freshly ground black pepper

Instructions:

1. Chop the peppers into small cubes, about 1/4 inch in size.
2. In a small bowl, combine the chopped peppers with the garlic, salt, olive oil, sugar, and pepper.
3. Mix the Ingredients together until everything is well combined.
4. Transfer the mixture to a clean, airtight container.
5. Cover the mixture and let it ferment in the refrigerator for 4 days.
6. Stir the mixture once or twice a day to evenly distribute the flavors.
7. Once the peppers have reached your desired level of fermentation, they are ready to enjoy!

Nutrition information: Per Serving (4 Servings): Calories: 84, Total Fat: 4.3 g, Saturated Fat: 0.6 g, Cholesterol: 0 mg, Carbohydrates: 9.8 g, Dietary Fiber: 2.2 g, Protein: 1.7 g, Potassium: 257.2 mg, Sodium: 853.5 mg

22. Fermented asparagus spears

Fermented asparagus spears is a delicious and easy-to-make recipe that will make you crave for more. This unique recipe combines the flavors of garlic, oregano, onions, and asparagus to create a crunchy and fermeted appetizer.
Serving: 4-6
Preparation time: 10 minutes

Ready time: 10 days

Ingredients:

- 2 pounds asparagus spears
- 1 teaspoon oregano
- 2 cloves of garlic, minced
- 1/2 onion, thinly sliced
- Salt
- 1 ½ cups of water
- 1 tablespoon of sugar
- 2 tablespoons of white vinegar

Instructions:

1. Trim asparagus spears, leaving about 3 – 4 inches from the top.
2. Place the asparagus in a glass jar.
3. Add garlic, oregano, and onion to the jar.
4. Dissolve the salt, sugar, and vinegar in the water and pour it over the asparagus, covering all Ingredients.
5. Seal jar with a lid.
6. Place jar in a warm, dry place for 10 days.

Nutrition Info (per serving):
Calories: 52
Fat: 0.4g
Carbohydrates: 9g
Fiber: 4g
Protein: 5.3g

23. Fermented zucchini rounds

Fermented zucchini rounds is a unique and flavorful fermented vegetable dish that is perfect as a side or topping for salads, sandwiches, tacos, or burgers. It's easy to make and is packed with probiotics!
Serving: 6 servings
Preparation Time: 15 minutes
Ready Time: 2-3 days

Ingredients:

-3 medium-sized zucchinis

-Sea salt
-3 cloves of garlic, minced
-1 teaspoon of dill weed
-1 teaspoon of black peppercorns
-½ cup of whey (optional)

Instructions:
1. Slice the zucchinis into thin rounds and place them in a medium-sized bowl.
2. Sprinkle the salt over the top of the zucchini rounds.
3. Mix the garlic, dill, and peppercorns together in a small bowl and sprinkle over the top of the zucchini rounds.
4. Place the zucchini rounds in a glass airtight container and cover with a lid.
5. Allow the mixture to sit for 2-3 days in a warm place.
6. Once the zucchini rounds have fermented, store them in the refrigerator.

Nutrition information:
Calories: 26
Fat: 0.1g
Carbohydrates: 5.9g
Fiber: 1.6g
Protein: 1.3g
Sugar: 2.9g

24. Fermented broccoli florets

Fermented broccoli florets is a delicious and nutritious side dish that is perfect for any meal. This dish is simple to make and is packed with vitamins, minerals and probiotics to help boost your health. The fermentation process gives the broccoli florets a tangy, garlicky flavor that is sure to turn heads.
Serving: 4
Preparation time: 10 minutes
Ready time: 4-5 days

Ingredients:

- 3 cups of broccoli florets
- 2 tablespoons of sea salt
- 3 cloves of garlic, minced
- 2 tablespoons of organic apple cider vinegar
- ¼ cup of water

Instructions:
1. In a glass jar, combine the broccoli florets, garlic and sea salt.
2. Mix together the apple cider vinegar and water, then pour over the broccoli florets.
3. Place a lid on the jar, then set in a warm spot for 4-5 days.
4. After 4-5 days, the fermentation process should be complete. Remove lid and enjoy!

Nutrition information:
Fermented broccoli contains vitamins A, C and K, calcium, fiber and probiotics. A single serving of approximately ¼ cup offers 3.3g of carbohydrates, 0.3 grams of fat and 0.5 grams of protein.

25. Fermented eggplant slices

Fermented eggplant slices provide an easy and unique way to enjoy the popular Asian vegetable. A combination of garlic, chili peppers, and spices gives this dish a unique flavor. It can be served as an appetizer, side dish, or part of a main course.
Serving: Makes 4-6 servings
Preparation time: 15 minutes
Ready time: 3-4 days

Ingredients:
• 2 eggplants
• 3 cloves of garlic
• 2-3 teaspoons of chili powder
• 2 teaspoons of sea salt
• 1 teaspoon of sugar
• 2 tablespoons of vinegar
• 2 tablespoons of oil

Instructions:
1. Cut the eggplants into thin slices about 1/4 inch thick.
2. Mince the garlic and combine with chili powder, sea salt and sugar in a medium bowl.
3. Drizzle the eggplant slices with the garlic and spice mixture, ensuring that all slices are evenly coated.
4. Place the eggplant slices in a sterilized glass jar and pour vinegar over them.
5. Let sit at room temperature for 3-4 days, turning the slices over periodically.
6. Once the eggplant is fermented, heat 2 tablespoons of oil in a skillet over medium heat.
7. Fry the eggplant slices in the oil until they are golden brown.
8. Serve warm as an appetizer, side dish, or part of a main course.

Nutrition information
Per Serving (Multiplied by 6): 188 Calories, 14.2g Fat, 11.1g Carbohydrates, 2.8g Protein

26. Fermented okra

Fermented okra is an easy-to-make fermented vegetables recipe that makes a delicious side dish with a tangy and spicy flavor.
Serving: 4-6
Preparation time: 10 minutes
Ready time: 1-2 days

Ingredients:
-2 lbs okra
-3 tablespoons sea salt
-Filtered water
-Optional spices (coriander, chili, garlic)

Instructions:
1. Wash the okra and then cut the stem ends.
2. Put the okra in a large bowl or jar and sprinkle with the salt.
3. Pound the mixture with a wooden spoon or pestle to release the juices from the okra.

4. Add the optional spices if desired and mix the Ingredients together.
5. Add filtered water to cover the okra and leave a few inches of space at the top of the container.
6. Cover the container and let the mixture ferment for 1-2 days at room temperature.
7. Taste the mixture after 1 day and then check for the desired taste. If it's too tart, let it ferment for another day and taste it again.
8. Once the desired flavor is reached, transfer the fermented okra to a jar with a lid and store in the refrigerator.

Nutrition information for fermented okra per serving (143g): Calories 61, Total fat 0g, Sodium 1660mg, Total Carbohydrate 9g, Dietary Fiber 3g, Sugars 0g, Protein 3g.

27. Fermented Brussels sprouts

Fermented Brussels sprouts are a unique and delicious way to enjoy traditional Brussels sprouts. The fermentation process creates a sweet and sour flavor that adds more depth and complexity to Brussels sprouts.
Serving: 4
Preparation Time: 10 minutes
Ready Time: 2 days

Ingredients:
- 1 pound of Brussels sprouts
- 2 tablespoons of sea salt
- 2 tablespoons of whey (or 1 teaspoon of probiotic powder)

Instructions:
1. Begin by washing the Brussels sprouts and trimming off any outer leaves.
2. Slice the Brussels sprouts into halves or quarters, depending on their size.
3. In a large bowl, combine the salt and whey (or probiotic powder), and mix to combine.
4. Add the Brussels sprouts to the bowl, and use your hands to massage the salt mixture into the sprouts.

5. Place the Brussels sprouts into a clean and sterilized jar, pressing them down firmly as you fill it.
6. Pour any remaining brine from the bowl over the sprouts, then top with a weight to submerge them in the brine.
7. Seal the jar tightly, and leave on countertop at room temperature for 1-2 days, until the desired sourness is achieved.
8. Transfer the jar to the refrigerator and enjoy!

Nutrition information (per serving):
Calories: 105 kcal, Carbohydrates: 11 g, Protein: 4 g, Fat: 0.2 g, Sodium: 696 mg, Fiber: 5 g

28. Fermented leeks

Fermented leeks are a great way to add a bit of tang and probiotic goodness to your diet. This recipe is easy to make and provides a delicious accompaniment to many dishes.
Serving: 4–6
Preparation Time: 15 minutes
Ready Time: 3 weeks

Ingredients:
- 2 large leeks
- 2 tablespoons Himalayan or sea salt
- 1 teaspoon sugar
- 2 tablespoons whey, optional

Instructions:
1. Clean the leeks thoroughly, being careful to remove any dirt or debris.
2. Cut the leeks into 1-inch thick circles, then place them in a large bowl.
3. Add the salt, sugar, and whey (if using) to the bowl and mix well.
4. Transfer the leeks to a glass jar and cover with a lid or cheesecloth.
5. Place the jar in a cool, dark place and leave to ferment for 2–3 weeks.
6. Taste a piece of leek every few days to check for desired sourness.
7. Once ready, store in the fridge and enjoy within two weeks.

Nutrition information: Per Serving: Calories: 30, Fat: 0g, Carbohydrates: 6g, Protein: 1g, Fiber: 1g, Sugar: 0g, Sodium: 600mg

29. Fermented sweet potato wedges

Fermented sweet potato wedges are an easy and delicious side dish- perfect for a dinner party or a weeknight meal. This recipe calls for sweet potatoes to be seasoned and slowly fermented in a salty brine, for a unique and tangy flavor that is sure to impress.
Serving: 6
Preparation Time: 10 minutes
Ready Time: 24 hours

Ingredients:
-2 lbs sweet potatoes, peeled and cut into wedges
-4 cups water
-1/4 cup sea salt

Instructions:
1. In a large bowl, mix together water and sea salt until the salt is dissolved.
2. Add the sweet potato wedges to the brine, and cover the bowl with a cloth.
3. Leave to ferment in a cool, dark place for 24 hours.
4. Serve as a side dish with a protein and vegetables.

Nutrition information:
Per Serving: 140 calories, 4g fat, 23g carbohydrate, 1g protein.

30. Fermented parsnip sticks

Fermented parsnip sticks are an easy to make and healthy snack option that can be enjoyed with any meal. With its great flavor and crispy texture, this snack will quickly become a favorite.
Serving: 4
Preparation Time: 10 minutes

Ready Time: 24 hours

Ingredients:
• 2 large parsnips
• 5 tablespoons of sea salt
• Water

Instructions:
1. Peel and wash the parsnips, then cut into strips
2. Place the strips into a glass jar and cover with 2 tablespoons of salt and fill with cold water.
3. Secure the lid and store the jar in a cool dark place for 24 hours.
4. After 24 hours has passed, drain the parsnips and cover with an additional 3 tablespoons of salt.
5. Place back into the cold dark spot and let sit for an additional 24 hours.
6. Drain the salt water, rinse the parsnips with filtered water and then spread evenly on a baking tray.
7. Preheat the oven to 350°F and bake for 10-15 minutes or until golden brown and crisp.
8. Serve and enjoy!

Nutrition information:
Serving size: 1/4 cup
Calories: 30
Total Fat: 0g
Sodium: 656mg
Carbohydrates: 6g
Sugars: 1g
Protein: 1g

31. Fermented butternut squash cubes

This is a simple, healthy, and delicious recipe for Fermented Butternut Squash Cubes. Fermentation is a great way to transform squash into something of a superfood, packed full of probiotics and beneficial enzymes.
Serving: Serves 4

Preparation time: 10 minutes
Ready time: 4 days

Ingredients:
• 2 cups peeled and cubed butternut squash
• 1 teaspoon sea salt
• 2 tablespoons apple cider vinegar
• Filtered water, as needed

Instructions:
1. Peel and cube the butternut squash and place in a medium-sized bowl.
2. Sprinkle the sea salt over the squash cubes and then add the apple cider vinegar and enough filtered water to cover the cubes.
3. Stir the mixture thoroughly to dissolve the salt and combine Ingredients.
4. Cover the bowl with a plate or towel and let sit for 4 days.
5. After 4 days, taste to see if the squash has reached your desired level of fermentation. If not, let ferment for another day.
6. Drain the liquid from the bowl and discard.
7. Store the fermented squash in a sealed container in the refrigerator.

Nutrition information:
One serving of Fermented Butternut Squash Cubes (2 cups) contains 86 calories, 2g of fat, 18g of carbohydrates, 4g of fiber, and 4g of protein.

32. Fermented radicchio leaves

Fermented radicchio leaves is an Italian dish that combines the bitterness of radicchio, the sweetness of herbs, and the savoriness of garlic in a nutritious and tasty salad.
Serving: 4
Preparation time: 15 minutes
Ready time: 15-24 hours

Ingredients:
- 4large radicchio leaves
- 1tablespoon olive oil
- 2garlic cloves, minced

- 2tablespoons mint leaves, chopped
- 1tablespoon oregano, chopped
- 2tablespoons parsley, chopped
- 1/4teaspoon sea salt

Instructions:
1. Wash the radicchio leaves and then pat them dry with paper towels.
2. In a large bowl, drizzle the radicchio leaves with the olive oil and gently rub them so the oil is evenly distributed.
3. Add the minced garlic, chopped mint, chopped oregano, and chopped parsley to the bowl and mix together.
4. Sprinkle the salt over the top and mix everything together once again.
5. Place the radicchio leaves in a mason jar or other air-tight container. Make sure that the mixture is evenly distributed among the leaves.
6. Cover the container with a lid and leave it at room temperature for 15-24 hours allowing it to ferment.
7. Once fermented to desired flavor, taste the leaves and adjust the seasoning if necessary. Enjoy!

Nutrition information: Per serving, this recipe provides: 114 calories, 7.6g of fat, 7.4g of carbohydrates, 4.6g of protein, and 1.2g of dietary fiber.

33. Fermented kale chips

Fermented kale chips are a flavorful and nutrition-packed snack made with kale and sea salt. They are crunchy, tangy and a great alternative from boring chips.
Serving: Makes 8 servings
Preparation time: 10 mins
Ready time: 24 hours

Ingredients:
• 150g Kale Leaves
• 2 tsp Sea Salt
• 500ml Water

Instructions:

1. Wash and clean the kale leaves.
2. Cut them into bite-sized chips and place in a large bowl.
3. Add sea salt and mix together.
4. Transfer chips to a large jar and fill with water until kale is completely covered.
5. Place a lid on the jar, but leave it slightly open.
6. Place the jar in a dark place and let ferment for at least 24 hours.
7. Check the chips every 8-10 hours, stirring and making sure kale is still submerged.
8. Taste a chip after 24 hours and decide if it's ready.
9. Once fermented, drain the chips and place on a paper towel to dry.
10. Store in an air tight container for up to 10 days.

Nutrition information:
• Calories: 28 kcal
• Fat: 0.4g
• Carbohydrate: 4.6g
• Protein: 1.6g
• Fiber: 0.9g
• Sodium: 301mg

34. Fermented turnip slices

Fermented turnip slices is a popular Chinese dish. It is made with fermented turnips, which gives it a unique texture and flavor. This dish can be served as either a side dish or a main meal.
Serving: 4
Preparation Time: 45 minutes
Ready Time: 90 minutes

Ingredients:
- 2 large turnips
- 2 tablespoons of vegetable oil
- 1 teaspoon of salt
- 2 tablespoons of sugar
- 2 teaspoons of grated ginger

Instructions:

1. Peel and slice the turnips into 1/2 inch thick slices.
2. Heat the oil in a pan over medium-high heat.
3. Add the turnips slices to the pan and season with salt and sugar.
4. Fry the turnips for 5 minutes until lightly golden-brown.
5. Add in the ginger and cook for an additional 2 minutes.
6. Reduce the heat to low and let the turnips simmer for 45 minutes.
7. Turn off the heat and let the turnips cool for 15 minutes.
8. Place the turnips in an airtight container and store in the refrigerator for 2 days.

Nutrition information: Serving size – 4, Calories – 108, Total Fat – 2 g, Cholesterol – 0 mg, Total Carbohydrates – 21 g, Dietary Fiber – 3 g, Sugars – 9 g, Protein – 2 g.

35. Fermented fennel bulbs

Fermented fennel bulbs make a wonderful savory addition to salads, sandwiches, and other meals and add a unique flavor to any dish. This recipe teaches you how to make delicious and easy fermented fennel bulbs in just a few steps.
Serving: 4
Preparation Time: 10 minutes
Ready Time: 3-4 days

Ingredients:
- 4 fennel bulbs, quartered
- 1 teaspoon sea salt
- 2 tablespoons apple cider vinegar
- Filtered water

Instructions:
1. Cut the fennel bulbs into quarters and add to a large jar.
2. Mix the sea salt and apple cider vinegar in a bowl and add to the jar.
3. Fill the jar with filtered water, ensuring the fennel is completely submerged.
4. Put the lid on the jar and place in a cool dark place for 3-4 days.
5. Drain and enjoy!

Nutrition information:
Calories: 50 kcal, Carbohydrates: 11 g, Protein: 2 g, Fat: 0 g, Saturated Fat: 0 g, Sodium: 58 mg, Potassium: 324 mg, Fiber: 6 g, Sugar: 3 g, Vitamin A: 20 IU, Vitamin C: 22 mg, Calcium: 44 mg, Iron: 1 mg

36. Fermented artichoke hearts

Fermented artichoke hearts are a delicious and nutritious Italian-style dish. The artichokes are marinated and fermented in a flavorful brine, creating a tangy and complex flavor.
Serving: 4
Preparation time: 10 minutes
Ready time: 4-5 days

Ingredients:
- 4 freshwater artichokes
- 2 tablespoons of sea salt
- ½ cup of filtered water
- 2 tablespoons of apple cider vinegar

Instructions:
1. Start by preparing the artichokes. Cut off the stem and remove any discolored or tough outer leaves. Once the artichokes are prepped, place them in a medium-sized bowl.
2. Make the brine by combining the sea salt, filtered water, and apple cider vinegar in a small bowl. Stir until the sea salt is dissolved.
3. Pour the brine over the artichokes and cover the bowl with a plate or towel. Let the artichokes sit for an hour.
4. Remove the plate or towel and transfer the artichokes into a fermenting vessel. Add enough of the brine to cover the artichokes completely.
5. Cover the vessel and let the artichokes ferment for 4-5 days, depending on taste.
6. Once the artichokes have fermented, store them in the refrigerator.

Nutrition information: Fermented artichoke hearts are a healthy, low-calorie snack. Each serving provides 1 gram of dietary fiber, 2 grams of protein, and 5 grams of carbohydrates.

37. Fermented pumpkin cubes

Fermented pumpkin cubes make a savory and flavorful addition to any meal as a side dish! This recipe uses only a few simple Ingredients but packs a big punch in flavor.
Serving: 4
Preparation time: 15 minutes
Ready time: 2 days

Ingredients:
- 2 lb pumpkin cubes
- 2 cloves garlic, minced
- 2 tbsp soy sauce
- 1 tsp salt
- 1 tbsp sugar
- 1 tsp red pepper flakes
- 1/2 cup water

Instructions:
1. Preheat oven to 375 degrees.
2. Place pumpkin cubes on a baking sheet and bake for 20 minutes, or until lightly browned.
3. In a medium-sized bowl, mix together garlic, soy sauce, salt, sugar, and red pepper flakes to make the marinade.
4. Toss the pumpkin cubes in the mixture and then transfer into a jar.
5. Add the water to the jar and seal.
6. Place jar in a cool and dark place and leave to ferment for 2 days.
7. After the fermentation is complete, remove the pumpkin cubes from the jar and serve.

Nutrition information: (per serving) Calories: 100, Total fat: 0g, Saturated fat: 0g, Sodium: 400mg, Carbohydrates: 22g, Fiber: 4g, Sugar: 11g, Protein: 3g

38. Fermented spinach dip

Fermented spinach dip is a flavorful, tangy dip that's packed with loads of nutrition. It's easy to make, super creamy, and is sure to be a hit at any gathering!
Serving: 8
Preparation Time: 15 minutes
Ready Time: 1 hour

Ingredients:
- 1 pound of fresh spinach
- 2 tablespoons of sugar
- ½ cup of plain yogurt
- 2 cloves of garlic, chopped
- ¼ teaspoon of sea salt
- 2 tablespoons of white vinegar
- ½ teaspoon of black pepper

Instructions:
1. Chop up your spinach and place it in a large bowl.
2. Add the sugar, yogurt, garlic, sea salt, vinegar, and black pepper.
3. Mix together until everything is evenly combined.
4. Cover the bowl with a damp paper towel and let it sit at room temperature for 1 hour.
5. After one hour, uncover the bowl, mix everything together, and taste. If you would like a stronger flavor, cover the bowl again and let it ferment for an additional hour.
6. Transfer the dip to a serving bowl, and enjoy!

Nutrition information: Per serving (1/8th of recipe): Calories: 46, Fat: 1g, Carbs: 7.9g, Protein: 2.4g, Sodium: 92.5mg, Fiber: 1.8g

39. Fermented celery sticks

Fermented celery sticks is a flavorful and nutrient-dense snack. This easy-to-make dish is perfect for any occasion.
Serving: 6-8
Preparation Time: 10 minutes
Ready Time: 4-5 days

Ingredients:
- 10-12 celery stalks, sliced or cut into thirds
- 2 cloves garlic, minced
- 2 tablespoons hot sauce
- 2 tablespoons sea salt
- 1 tablespoon honey
- Filtered water

Instructions:
1. In a clean 1-quart jar, mix together the garlic, hot sauce, honey, and salt.
2. Fill the jar with filtered water until the celery stalks are completely covered.
3. Place the jar in a warm spot in the kitchen and cover the jar with a towel to keep monitor the temperature.
4. Make sure to check on the celery every day for the next 4-5 days.
5. After 4-5 days, test the fermentation by tasting the celery stick.
6. Once you're happy with the fermentation, strain the liquid from the jar and store the celery sticks in the refrigerator.

Nutrition information: Fermented celery sticks are a great source of vitamin K, as well as dietary fibers. It also contains calcium, manganese, copper, iron, magnesium, zinc, potassium, and more. They are low in calories and fat, and are considered to be a great addition to any healthy diet.

40. Fermented watermelon radishes

Fermented watermelon radishes are a unique and tasty snack that is crisp and slightly sour in flavor. They are made by soaking whole radishes in a brine-based mixture. This creates a delicious and slightly acidic product, perfect for snacking on.
Serving: Makes 2 cups of fermented watermelon radishes.
Preparation Time: 10 minutes
Ready Time: 7-10 days

Ingredients:
· 4 watermelon radishes

· 4 teaspoons of sea salt
· 2 cups of filtered water

Instructions:
1. Start by washing the watermelon radishes.
2. Cut them into small cubes about ½ inch thick.
3. In a clean jar add the cubed watermelon radiator, sea salt and filtered water.
4. Secure the lid and shake the jar until the salt is dissolved.
5. Place the jar in a cool place out of direct sunlight and let it sit for 7-10 days.
6. Open the jar daily to let any built-up gas escape.
7. Once ready, strain the liquid and store the watermelon radishes in the fridge for up to one month.

Nutrition information (Per Serving):
· Calories: 23 kcal
· Carbohydrates: 5.6 g
· Protein: 0.6 g
· Fat: 0.1 g

41. Fermented mushroom medley

Fermented mushroom medley is a savory, flavorful dish that can be served as either an appetizer or a side dish. It contains a combination of mushrooms that are naturally fermented with seasonings to bring out the unique flavor.
Serving: Makes 4 servings
Preparation Time: 15 minutes
Ready Time: 3-5 hours

Ingredients:
• 8 ounces of mixed mushrooms such as shiitake, oyster, cremini, and white button
• 2 tablespoons of extra virgin olive oil
• 1 teaspoon of sea salt
• ½ teaspoon of black pepper
• 2 cloves of minced garlic

• 1 teaspoon of fresh thyme leaves
• 2 tablespoons of white wine

Instructions:
1. In a medium bowl, combine the mushrooms with the olive oil, salt and pepper.
2. Heat a large skillet over medium heat. Add the mushrooms and sauté for 5 minutes or until slightly softened.
3. Add the garlic and stir to combine. Cook for 1 minute.
4. Add the white wine and thyme leaves. Cook for 2 minutes.
5. Place the mushroom mixture in a glass jar with a lid and let stand at room temperature for 3-5 hours.
6. Serve warm or at room temperature.

Nutrition information:
• Calories: 45
• Protein: 2.3g
• Carbohydrates: 5.3g
• Fat: 2.2g
• Sodium: 254mg

42. Fermented green tomato relish

Fermented green tomato relish is a delicious condiment that features a unique flavor and is perfect for serving with sandwiches, salads, and more.
Serving: Makes 4 cups
Preparation time: 20 minutes
Ready time: 5 days

Ingredients:
- 4 cups green tomatoes, chopped
- ¼ cup sea salt
- ¼ cup raw apple cider vinegar
- 1 teaspoon sugar
- 2 cloves garlic, minced
- 2 tablespoons freshly grated ginger
- 2 teaspoons dried oregano

- 2 teaspoons chili powder

Instructions:
1. Place the chopped tomatoes in a large bowl and sprinkle with the salt. Mix together until combined and let sit for about 10 minutes.
2. Transfer the salted tomatoes to a glass jar. Add the apple cider vinegar, sugar, garlic, ginger, oregano, and chili powder.
3. Cover the jar with a lid and shake well to combine.
4. Place the jar in a cool, dark place and let sit for 5 days. Shake the jar every day to help mix the flavors and promote fermentation.
5. After 5 days, the relish is ready. Store in the refrigerator for up to 3 weeks.

Nutrition information: Each 2-tablespoon serving of the fermented green tomato relish contains 16 calories, 783 milligrams of sodium, and 2 grams of carbohydrates.

43. Fermented pickled onions

Fermented pickled onions are a classic addition to sandwiches, tacos, salads and burgers. They offer a tart and tangy flavor, making them a popular condiment. It's easy to make your own fermented pickled onions at home with just a few Ingredients.
Serving: 4-6
Preparation Time: 10 minutes
Ready Time: 1-2 days

Ingredients:
• 5-6 Medium White Onion, thinly sliced
• 4 cups Water
• 2 tablespoons Salt
• 2 tablespoons Raw Apple Cider Vinegar
• 2 tablespoons Honey

Instructions:
1. Thinly slice the onions and place in a large bowl.
2. Combine water, salt, apple cider vinegar, and honey in a measuring cup.

3. Pour over onions.
4. Let sit for 10 minutes to allow the onions to soften.
5. Transfer the onions and the liquid to a large glass jar.
6. Tightly close the lid on the jar and let sit at room temperature for 1-2 days for best results.
7. Refrigerate and enjoy!

Nutrition information: Serving size: 1/4 cup; Calories: 40; Total Fat: 0g; Cholesterol: 0mg; Sodium: 460mg; Total Carbohydrates: 9g; Fiber: 1g; Sugars: 4g; Protein: 1g.

44. Fermented carrot and daikon radish slaw

This delicious fermented carrot and daikon radish slaw is easy to make and has a tangy and sweet flavor. Not only is it tasty, but it's also packed with probiotics and vitamins, making it a great addition to any meal.
Serving: 4
Preparation Time: 10 minutes
Ready Time: 2-3 days

Ingredients:
- 2 medium carrots, grated
- 1 small daikon radish, grated
- 2 tablespoons coarse sea salt
- 2 tablespoons honey
- 2 tablespoons apple cider vinegar
- 2 cups filtered water

Instructions:
1. In a large bowl, combine grated carrots and daikon radish.
2. Add sea salt, honey, apple cider vinegar, and filtered water. Stir to combine.
3. Transfer mixture to a mason jar or other airtight container.
4. Cover the jar with a tight-fitting lid and let sit on the countertop for 2-3 days to allow fermentation to occur.
5. When the fermentation process is complete, transfer to the refrigerator and enjoy as a side dish or topping on salads and sandwiches.

Nutrition information: Per serving, this fermented carrot and daikon radish slaw contains 70 calories, 6 grams of carbohydrates, 2 grams of protein, and 3.5 grams of fat.

45. Fermented roasted peppers

Fermented roasted peppers is a flavorful dish that's easy to make. This recipe combines roasted sweet peppers with lactic-acid fermentation to create a creamy, savory side dish.
Serving: 6
Preparation Time: 15 minutes
Ready Time: 5-7 days

Ingredients:
• 6-8 sweet peppers
• 2 tablespoons of sea salt
• 2 tablespoons of honey
• 2 cups of filtered water

Instructions:
1. Preheat oven to 350°F (177°C).
2. Place the sweet peppers on a baking sheet and roast in preheated oven for 10-15 minutes.
3. Remove from oven and let cool.
4. Cut the roasted peppers into thin strips.
5. Place the pepper strips in a sterilized glass jar, making sure to leave some space at the top.
6. In a bowl, mix together the sea salt, honey, and water.
7. Pour the mixture into the jar over the peppers, making sure they are completely submerged in the liquid.
8. Place a lid on the jar and let ferment in a cool, dry place for 5-7 days.
9. After the peppers are done fermenting, store them in the refrigerator.

Nutrition information: Per Serving (2 oz): Calories: 191, Protein: 3g, Total Fat: 1.3g, Total Carbohydrates: 43.2g, Dietary Fiber: 10.3g, Sugar: 11.1g, Sodium: 1920mg.

46. Fermented rutabaga fries

Fermented Rutabaga Fries are a savory and tasty side dish that is sure to be a hit at any gathering. Made with fermented rutabagas and herbs, these fries are a great way to add flavor to any meal.
Serving: 4-6
Preparation time: 15 minutes
Ready time: 45 minutes

Ingredients:
- 2 medium rutabagas, peeled and cut into wedges
- 2 tablespoons olive oil
- 1 teaspoon sea salt
- 1/4 teaspoon black pepper
- 2 cloves garlic, chopped
- 2 tablespoons fresh herbs (such as oregano, thyme, or rosemary), chopped

Instructions:
1. Preheat oven to 400F.
2. Line a baking sheet with parchment paper.
3. In a large bowl, combine rutabaga wedges, olive oil, sea salt, black pepper, garlic and herbs. Mix until the rutabaga wedges are fully coated.
4. Spread the rutabaga wedges onto the baking sheet, making sure to spread them out in a single layer.
5. Bake in preheated oven for 30-35 minutes, flipping halfway, until the rutabaga wedges are crispy and golden.
6. Serve warm and enjoy!

Nutrition information: Serving size: 1/6 of the recipe; Calories: 114; Total fat: 7g; Cholesterol: 0mg; Sodium: 277mg; Total carbohydrates: 12g; Sugars: 5g; Protein: 1g

47. Fermented snap peas

Fermented snap peas are a delicious and healthy snack or side dish. This recipe is easy to make and packs a flavorful punch.
Serving: 6

Preparation time: 15 minutes
Ready time: 2 weeks

Ingredients:
- 2 cups of snap peas
- 2 tablespoons of kosher salt
- 2 tablespoons of sugar
- 2 tablespoons of red pepper
- 2 tablespoons of chopped garlic
- 2 tablespoons of chopped onion
- 1 cup of filtered water

Instructions:
1. In a bowl, mix the salt and sugar together.
2. Place the snap peas in a glass jar and pour the salt and sugar mixture over them.
3. Add the red pepper, garlic, and onion to the jar and mix to combine.
4. Pour the filtered water into the jar until the peas are fully submerged.
5. Place a lid on the jar and let it sit at room temperature in a dark place for 2 weeks.
6. During this time, open the jar and stir the contents once a day to ensure even fermentation.
7. Once the two weeks have passed, your fermented snap peas are ready to enjoy!

Nutrition information:
- Per Serving (1/6 batch) - Calories: 34, Total Fat: 0g, Sodium: 348mg, Potassium: 68mg, Carbohydrates: 7g, Dietary Fiber: 2g, Sugars: 2g, Protein: 2g

48. Fermented radish and beet salad

This colorful and flavorful Fermented Radish and Beet Salad is a true specialty, made of healthy natural Ingredients that blend together in a well-balanced way. It's crunchy, refreshing, and rich in flavor and vitamins.
Serving: 4-6
Preparation time: 20 minutes

Ready time: 1 hour

Ingredients:
•1 large radish, grated
•1 red beet, grated
•1 teaspoon apple cider vinegar
•1 teaspoon olive oil
•2 cloves garlic, minced
•1 teaspoon salt
•½ teaspoon dill, fresh
•1 teaspoon black peppercorns

Instructions:
1. In a bowl, mix the grated radish and red beet together and set aside.
2. In a second bowl, add the apple cider vinegar, olive oil, minced garlic, salt, fresh dill, and black peppercorns and use a whisk to blend the mixture together.
3. Pour the mixture over the radish and beets and mix until well combined.
4. Place the salad in a glass jar, cover securely, and store in the refrigerator for 1 hour.
5. Serve the fermented radish and beet salad cold.

Nutrition information:
Calories: 42
Fat: 2.5g
Carbohydrates: 4.5g
Protein: 1.5g
Sodium: 428mg
Fiber: 1g

49. Fermented green chili salsa

Fermented green chili salsa is a spicy, flavorful condiment that can be used to top off tacos, burritos, or eaten as a dip.
Serving: 6 servings
Preparation time: 15 minutes
Ready time: 17-20 hours

Ingredients:
- 4-5 fresh green chilies, stems removed and halved
- ½ cup sea salt
- 2 cloves garlic, finely minced
- ½ cup filtered water
- 2 tablespoons apple cider vinegar

Instructions:
1. Place the chilies in a clean glass jar or fermentation vessel.
2. Mix the sea salt with the garlic, and then stir in the water and apple cider vinegar until the salt is dissolved.
3. Pour the brine into the jar with the chilies, making sure that the chilies are completely submerged.
4. Place a weight inside the jar to keep the chilies submerged and seal the jar.
5. Keep the jar at room temperature to ferment for 17-20 hours.
6. Taste the salsa and if it is to your liking, discard any sediment in the bottom, and transfer the salsa to an airtight glass container.

Nutrition information: Per serving, Fermented Green Chili Salsa contains 30 calories, 1g of protein, 1g of fat, 5g of carbohydrate, 2g of dietary fiber, and 220mg of sodium.

50. Fermented onion jam

Fermented onion jam is a savory jam that combines traditional jam-making techniques with a fermentation-based process for an interesting flavor profile. It can be used in a variety of dishes, or served on its own as a condiment.

Serving: Makes approximately 3 servings

Preparation Time: 10 minutes

Ready Time: 24 hours

Ingredients:
- 2 large onions, sliced
- 2 tablespoons olive oil
- 1 teaspoon fine sea salt

- 1/8 teaspoon sugar
- 2 tablespoons raw apple cider vinegar
- 2 tablespoons filtered water

Instructions:

1. Preheat your oven to 350°F.
2. Place the onion slices onto a baking sheet. Drizzle with the olive oil, and sprinkle with the salt and sugar. Mix everything together until the onions are evenly coated.
3. Bake for 10-15 minutes, or until the onions are lightly browned.
4. In a medium-sized bowl, combine the baked onions with the apple cider vinegar and water. Mix everything together until the onions are evenly coated.
5. Place the onion mixture into a mason jar. Cover the jar with a lid, and let it sit at room temperature for 24 hours, stirring occasionally.
6. After 24 hours, the onions will have fermented and turned into a jam-like consistency. Serve as desired.

Nutrition information:

Serving Size: 2 tablespoons (30g)
Calories: 25
Fat: 2g
Carbohydrates: 5g
Protein: 0g
Sugars: 3g

51. Fermented garlic dill green beans

Fermented garlic dill green beans is a delicious and healthy way to enjoy the flavor of these green beans. This recipe is ideal for those who like to try something different on special occasions. It has a unique flavor that goes well with a variety of dishes.
Serving: 4
Preparation Time: 10 mins
Ready Time: 3-5 days

Ingredients:

-2 pounds of green beans, washed and trimmed

-4 cloves of garlic, minced
-1 tablespoon of sea salt
-1 teaspoon of dill weed
-2 cups of purified water

Instructions:

1. In a glass jar, combine green beans, minced garlic, sea salt, and dill weed.
2. Fill the jar with purified water, leaving an inch or two of free space at the top.
3. Seal the jar and place it in a cool, dry place for 3-5 days for the fermentation process.
4. Once fermentation is complete, place the jar in the refrigerator.

Nutrition information: Serving size: 1 cup; Calories: 55; Total Fat: 0g; Cholesterol: 0mg; Sodium: 600mg; Total Carbohydrates: 8g; Dietary Fiber: 3g; Protein: 2g.

52. Fermented asparagus pickles

Fermented asparagus pickles are a unique take on traditional pickles and are a great way to add flavor and probiotic benefits to your diet.
Serving: Makes 4-5 pint jars
Preparation Time: 1 day
Ready Time: 14 days

Ingredients:

- 1 bunch of asparagus (1-2 lbs)
- 2 cloves of garlic, chopped
- 2 bay leaves
- 1 Tbsp sea salt
- 5-6 cloves (or 1/4 tsp ground cloves)
- 5-6 peppercorns (or 1/4 tsp ground pepper)
- 1 quart filtered water
- 2-3 Tbsp Pickle Crisp (optional)
- 1/4-1/2 cup non-chlorinated brine

Instructions:

1. Clean and trim the asparagus. You can slice or chop the asparagus into bite-sized pieces.
2. Place the asparagus in a glass, ceramic, or plastic (BPA free) container.
3. Add the garlic, bay leaves, sea salt, cloves, and peppercorns.
4. Bring the water to a boil, and then pour it over the asparagus.
5. Add the Pickle Crisp (if desired), and stir to combine.
6. Cover with a lid or plate, and place the container in a cool location. Leave the asparagus to ferment for 7-14 days, stirring every few days.
7. Once the asparagus has fermented to your liking, strain the mixture and add the brine.
8. Transfer the asparagus and brine to sterile jars. Store in the refrigerator for up to 3 months.

Nutrition information: Serving size 1/4 cup; Calories 10, Total Fat 0.2g, Sodium 271mg, Total Carbohydrate 2g, Dietary Fiber 1.3g, Protein 1.3g.

53. Fermented cucumber kimchi

Fermented cucumber kimchi is a spicy, flavorful and tangy Korean condiment made by fermenting cucumber and chili powder.
Serving: 4
Preparation time: 40 minutes
Ready time: 2 days

Ingredients:
- 2 large cucumbers
- 2 tablespoons coarse salt
- 2 tablespoons chili pepper flakes
- 2 tablespoons salted shrimp flakes
- 2 tablespoons minced garlic
- 2 tablespoons minced ginger
- 1 small apple, grated
- 3 tablespoons fish sauce
- 1 teaspoon sugar
- 4 tablespoons sesame oil
- 4 tablespoons white vinegar

Instructions:

1. Cut the cucumbers into thick spears or slices. Sprinkle with salt and let sit in a colander for 30 minutes. Rinse and drain.
2. In a medium bowl, combine chili pepper flakes, salted shrimp flakes, minced garlic, minced ginger, grated apple, fish sauce, sugar, sesame oil, and white vinegar.
3. In a separate bowl, mix together cucumbers and the chili pepper mixture.
4. Place cucumber mixture in a jar and cover with a lid. Let ferment at room temperature in a dark place for 1 to 2 days, until flavor is to your liking.

Nutrition information: per serving of 240g Fermented cucumber kimchi provide - Calories: 72kcal, Carbohydrates: 8g, Protein: 2g, Fat: 6g, Sodium: 1867mg, Potassium: 136mg, Fiber: 1g, Vitamin A: 206IU, Vitamin C: 7mg, Calcium: 8mg, Iron: 0.6mg.

54. Fermented ginger green beans

Fermented ginger green beans are a tasty and nutritious dish that combines the health benefits of ginger with the crunch of green beans. Rich in antioxidants, vitamins, and nutrients, this fermented dish is a delicious way to get your daily dose of greens.
Serving: 4
Preparation time: 10 minutes
Ready time: 3-5 days

Ingredients:

- 2 lbs. of green beans, trimmed
- 2 tablespoons of grated ginger
- 1 cup of whey or brine from a previous batch of fermentation
- 2 tablespoons of sea salt

Instructions:

1. In a large bowl, mix the green beans, grated ginger, whey or brine, and sea salt together until fully combined.
2. Place the mixture in a fermentation jar, filling up to two-thirds of the jar's capacity.

3. Place the lid on the jar and lightly close it.
4. Over the next 3-5 days, open the lid briefly each day to allow air to escape, then close it again.
5. After 3-5 days, the fermentation process should be complete and the ginger green beans should be ready to enjoy.

Nutrition information: Each serving of fermented ginger green beans contains 0g fat, 6g protein, 5g carbohydrates, and 95mg sodium.

55. Fermented roasted eggplant dip

Fermented roasted eggplant dip is a delicious and flavorful combination of smoked eggplant, garlic, spices, and yogurt. This dip is a great healthy snack or appetizer, and goes well with veggies, chips, and crackers.
Serving: Makes 4-6 servings.
Preparation Time: 15 minutes
Ready Time: 15 minutes

Ingredients:
-1 large smoked eggplant
-2 cloves garlic
-1/2 teaspoon ground cumin
-1/2 teaspoon smoked paprika
-1 teaspoon dried oregano
-1/4 cup Greek yogurt
-1 tablespoon olive oil
-Salt and pepper to taste

Instructions:
1. Preheat oven to 375 F (190 C).
2. Place the smoked eggplant on a sheet pan and roast in the oven for 15 minutes.
3. Mince the garlic and place in a bowl with the cumin, paprika, oregano, yogurt,and olive oil. Mix together.
4. Once the eggplant is done roasting, peel and mash with a fork and combine with the garlic and spice mixture.
5. Season with salt and pepper to taste

6. Serve with veggies, chips, and crackers.

Nutrition information: Per serving: Calories 164, Total Fat 10.6 g, Saturated Fat 2.1 g, Sodium 132 mg, Total Carbohydrates 14.9 g, Dietary Fiber 6.2 g, Protein 3.3 g

56. Fermented turmeric carrots

Fermented turmeric carrots are a delicious, spicy summer snack made from flavorful carrots and turmeric. The fermentation process enhances the flavors of both Ingredients to create a unique and memorable taste.
Serving: 8
Preparation time: 10 minutes
Ready time: 2 days

Ingredients:
- 2 lbs carrots
- 1 teaspoon turmeric
- 1/2 teaspoon both black pepper and sea salt
- 1 tablespoon honey
- 1 quart filtered water

Instructions:
1. Cut the carrots into thin strips or small cubes.
2. Place them into a medium-sized bowl and sprinkle with the turmeric, black pepper, and sea salt.
3. Drizzle the honey over the carrots and mix well.
4. Place the carrots into a jar or other fermentation vessel and pour the filtered water over them.
5. Cover the jar and place in a warm place for two days to ferment.
6. Transfer the jar to the refrigerator for storage.

Nutrition information:
Fermented turmeric carrots are a nutrient-dense snack that is low in fat and calorie-free. They are loaded with fiber, vitamin A, vitamin C, manganese, potassium, and iron. Additionally, the fermentation process preserves the health benefits of both the carrots and turmeric.

57. Fermented pepperoncini

Fermented pepperoncini is a traditional Mediterranean dish that is full of flavor and aroma. This dish is made with fresh pepperoncini peppers that are pickled in a brine and fermented, creating a spicy and delightful condiment.
Serving: This dish can be served as an accompaniment to sandwiches, salads, pasta dishes, and various types of meats.
Preparation time: 15 minutes
Ready time: 3 days

Ingredients:
• 2 cups of pepperoncini peppers
• 2 cloves of garlic, minced
• 2 tablespoons of sea salt
• 2 tablespoons of sugar
• 1 teaspoon of dried oregano
• 2 cups of water

Instructions:
1. Rinse the pepperoncini peppers and remove any stems or bruised peppers. Place the peppers in a large jar or bowl.
2. In a separate bowl, combine the minced garlic, salt, sugar, oregano, and water. Stir until all the Ingredients are fully incorporated.
3. Pour the brine mixture over the peppers, ensuring that the peppers are fully submerged.
4. Place a lid on the jar and leave it in a cool, dark place for at least 3 days, ensuring that the peppers remain submerged in the brine.
5. After 3 days, remove the lid and taste the pepperoncinis. If desired, they can be left to ferment for an additional 1-2 days for a deeper flavor.

Nutrition information:
Per serving size (1/4 cup): 25 calories, 0g fat, 330mg sodium, 6g carbohydrates, 1g fiber, 3g sugar, and 1g protein.

58. Fermented collard greens

Fermented collard greens are a delicious way to enjoy the antioxidant-rich superfood. This easy, fuss-free preparation takes only a few days and tastes great served with cooked grains or as part of a raw food meal.
Serving: Makes 4-6 servings
Preparation Time: 10 minutes
Ready Time: 5-6 days

Ingredients:
• 3 cups coarsely chopped collard greens
• 2 tsp. salt
• 1 tsp. ground black pepper
• 2 tbsp. apple cider vinegar

Instructions:
1. In a medium bowl, combine the collard greens, salt, pepper, and apple cider vinegar and toss to combine.
2. Transfer the mixture into a quart-sized jar and press down firmly to compress.
3. Fill the jar with room temperature filtered water, leaving about 1 inch of space from the top.
4. Cover the jar with a cheesecloth and secure with a rubber band.
5. Allow the mixture to ferment for 5-6 days in a cool, dark place, checking daily to release any built up gas pressure and stirring the contents.
6. Once the fermenting is complete, cover the jar with an airtight lid and store in the refrigerator.

Nutrition information: Per serving: 80 calories, 3g fat, 750mg sodium, 11g carbohydrates, 3g fiber, 5g sugar, 2g protein

59. Fermented cherry tomato salsa

This flavorful fermented cherry tomato salsa is the perfect accompaniment to a variety of dishes. The fermentation process gives it a unique flavor and offers probiotic benefits.
Serving: 6-8
Preparation Time: 10 minutes
Ready Time: 48 hours

Ingredients:
- 2 cups chopped cherry tomatoes
- 1/4 cup finely chopped onion
- 2 cloves garlic, grated
- 1-2 chillies, finely chopped
- 2 tablespoons olive oil
- 1/2 teaspoon sea salt
- 1/8 teaspoon ground black pepper

Instructions:
1. In a medium-size bowl, combine the tomatoes, onion, garlic, chillies, olive oil, salt and pepper.
2. Mix everything together thoroughly and transfer the mixture to a 1 quart mason jar or other fermentation container.
3. Secure the lid and place the container in a warm place to ferment for up to 48 hours.
4. Once the desired fermentation time has passed, open the lid and enjoy your homemade fermented cherry tomato salsa.

Nutrition information: Per serving (about 1/8 cup): Calories: 28, Fat: 2g, Saturated fat: 0.3g, Unsaturated fat: 1.7g, Carbohydrates: 3g, Sugar: 2g, Sodium: 262mg, Fiber: 1g, Protein: 1g, Cholesterol: 0mg

60. Fermented dilly beans

Fermented dilly beans are a popular snack made with green beans and a variety of herbs and spices. The fermentation process enhances the flavor, making them a tasty treat and a healthy source of probiotics.
Serving: Makes 1 cup
Preparation time: 10 minutes
Ready time: 24-48 hours

Ingredients:
- 1 cup green beans, trimmed and halved
- 1/4 teaspoon pink Himalayan salt
- 2 cloves garlic, minced

• 2 tablespoons dill, chopped
• 1 tablespoon apple cider vinegar
• 2 tablespoons filtered water

Instructions:
1. Add the green beans to a glass jar and sprinkle with salt.
2. Add the garlic, dill, vinegar, and water.
3. Secure the lid and shake the jar so the Ingredients are evenly mixed.
4. Place the jar in a warm location and let sit for 24-48 hours.
5. After the fermentation period, transfer to the refrigerator and store for up to 2 weeks.

Nutrition information: Per serving: Calories: 18; Fat: 0g; Sodium: 80mg; Carbs: 4g; Fiber: 1g; Protein: 1g.

61. Fermented cauliflower rice

Fermented cauliflower rice is a delicious and healthy spin on the classic rice dish. It is low in carbs, has a delicious umami-rich flavor and provides a range of nutrients to help boost immunity.
Serving: 6
Preparation Time: 15 minutes
Ready Time: 8-10 days

Ingredients:
• 1 head of cauliflower, grated
• 2 teaspoons sea salt
• 2 tablespoons of whey or ¼ teaspoon of starter culture
• ¼ cup of room temperature filtered water

Instructions:
1. Place the grated cauliflower in a large bowl and sprinkle with the sea salt.
2. Massage the salt into the cauliflower until it begins to soften and liquid is released.
3. Rinse the cauliflower under cool water and gently squeeze out any excess liquid.

4. Place the cauliflower back into the bowl and add the whey or starter culture and water.
5. Combine the Ingredients together until everything is fully incorporated.
6. Place the mixture into a wide-mouth mason jar and press down the cauliflower gently with a wooden spoon to ensure the vegetables are submerged in liquid.
7. Place the lid on the jar and store at room temperature out of direct sunlight for 8-10 days, depending on the environment.
8. After 8-10 days, open the lid and taste the mixture – it should be slightly sour.
9. If the desired flavor has not been achieved, leave it to ferment in the jar for a few more days.
10. Once the desired tartness has been achieved, transfer the jar to the refrigerator and enjoy your fermented cauliflower rice.

Nutrition information: Serving size 1/6 of the recipe. Calories: 33, Fat: 0.1g, Saturated Fat: 0.03g, Cholesterol: 0mg, Sodium: 298mg, Carbohydrates: 6.4g, Fiber: 2g, Sugar: 2.4g, Protein: 2.4g

62. Fermented pickled ginger

Fermented pickled ginger is a delicious condiment often served with sushi. It can be used as a garnish on salads or noodle dishes. With a slight vinegar spice and savory aroma, this dish is a delightful addition to many meals.
Serving: 4
Preparation time: 5 minutes
Ready time: 7 days

Ingredients:
• 2 cups fresh ginger, cut into paper thin slices
• 1/2 cup white sugar
• 1 teaspoon sea salt
• 2 tablespoons rice wine vinegar
• 2 cups warm water

Instructions:

1. In a bowl, mix together the sugar, salt, and vinegar.
2. Place the ginger slices into a glass jar and add the sugar mixture.
3. Pour the warm water into the jar to cover the ginger slices.
4. Seal jar and leave at room temperature for at least 7 days, turning the jar over every day.
5. After 7 days, remove the ginger slices from the jar and enjoy.

Nutrition information: Serving size: 1/4 cup, Calories: 55, Total Fat: 0.2 g, Cholesterol 0 mg, Sodium: 372 mg, Total Carbohydrate: 13.8 g, Protein: 0.6 g

63. Fermented jicama sticks

Fermented jicama sticks are a traditional Mexican snack that have been enjoyed for generations and that have been given a modern twist by incorporating different flavors and Ingredients. It is a crunchy, tongue-tickling, slightly tangy snack that is sure to delight.
Serving: Serves 4 people
Preparation time: 20 minutes
Ready time: 4 days

Ingredients:
• 2 lbs. of jicama, peeled and cut into 3-inch sticks
• 2 tablespoons of sea salt
• 2 tablespoons of sugar
• 2 cups of warm filtered water
• ¼ cup of starter culture

Instructions:
1. Combine the sea salt and sugar in a small bowl.
2. Place the jicama sticks in a 1-gallon jar and pour in the warm water.
3. Add the salt and sugar, stirring until it is fully dissolved.
4. Add the starter culture and stir again.
5. Secure the lid on the jar and let it sit at room temperature for 4 days.
6. Pour the mixture into a bowl and discard the used starter culture.
7. Rinse the jicama sticks under cold water.
8. Place the jicama sticks on a baking sheet and let them dry overnight, or until they are dry to the touch.

Nutrition information: Per serving: 95 calories, 0g fat, 21g carbohydrates, 1g protein, 5g dietary fiber

64. Fermented red onion relish

Fermented Red Onion Relish is a tasty and simple condiment that's easy to make and adds a unique flavor to your meals.
Serving: approximately 1-1/2 cups
Preparation Time: 10 minutes
Ready Time: 10 days

Ingredients:
- 4 red onions, chopped
- ½ cup apple cider vinegar
- 2 tablespoons sea salt
- 4 garlic cloves, minced
- 2 tablespoons honey
- 1 teaspoon red pepper flakes

Instructions:
1. Place the chopped onions in a glass or ceramic bowl and mix with the rest of the ingredients.
2. Put the bowl in an airtight container and leave at room temperature for 10 days.
3. After 10 days, the relish is done fermenting and can be stored in the refrigerator for up to 1 month.

Nutrition information: Serving size 1/4 cup, Calories 40, Total Fat 0 g, Cholesterol 0 mg, Sodium 433 mg, Total Carbohydrate 9 g, Dietary Fiber 1 g, Protein 1 g.

65. Fermented carrot ginger slaw

Fermented carrot ginger slaw is a healthy and delicious side dish. It has a crispy texture and a mix of sweet and tangy flavors.
Serving: 4 servings

Preparation time: 10 minutes
Ready time: 10 minutes

Ingredients:
- 4 cups grated carrots
- 2 tablespoons freshly grated ginger
- 2 tablespoons apple cider vinegar
- 3 tablespoons coconut sugar
- 1 teaspoon sea salt

Instructions:
1. In a large bowl, combine the grated carrots and ginger.
2. Add the apple cider vinegar, coconut sugar, and sea salt and mix until everything is evenly distributed.
3. Transfer the slaw to a sealable container, cover with a lid, and set aside for 10 minutes so that it can ferment.
4. After 10 minutes, the slaw is ready to be served.

Nutrition information: Per serving: 75 calories, 0 g fat, 18 g carbohydrates, 2 g protein, 4 g dietary fiber, 240 mg sodium

66. Fermented pickled radish and carrot salad

Fermented pickled radish and carrot salad is a flavorful and refreshing dish that is perfect to enjoy at any time of year. This salad is a combination of sweet and vaorful radish and carrots, which are pickled and fermented, giving them a unique flavor profile.
Serving: 4
Preparation time: 10 minutes
Ready time: 10-12 hours

Ingredients:
• 1 cup radishes, sliced thin
• 1 cup carrots, sliced thin
• 1/4 cup apple cider vinegar
• 2 tablespoons honey
• 1 teaspoon salt
• 1 teaspoon black peppercorns

• 1 tablespoon dried dill
• 1 teaspoon red chili flakes (optional)

Instructions:
1. In a bowl, combine the radishes and carrots.
2. In a separate bowl, mix together the apple cider vinegar, honey, salt, peppercorns, dill, and chili flakes until combined.
3. Pour the mixture over the vegetables and mix until everything is coated.
4. Cover the bowl with plastic wrap and let it sit in the refrigerator to pickle and ferment for 10-12 hours.
5. Once the vegetables have pickled and fermented, they are ready to eat!

Nutrition information: Per Serving: Calories: 88, Total Fat: 0.3g, Sodium: 398mg, Total Carbohydrate: 18.1g, Dietary Fiber: 2.4g, Protein: 1.8g

67. Fermented cherry pepper relish

Fermented cherry pepper relish is a delicious condiment that combines the sweet yet spicy taste of cherry peppers with the tangy flavor of fermentation. It's a great addition to sandwiches, salads, burgers, and more!
Serving: Makes about 2 cups of relish.
Preparation Time: 35 minutes
Ready Time: 2-4 weeks

Ingredients:
- 2 cups freshly picked sweet cherry peppers, roughly chopped
- 2 cups white wine vinegar
- 1 cup lukewarm filtered water
- 2 tablespoons sea salt
- 2 tablespoons honey

Instructions:
1. In a non-reactive bowl, mix together cherry peppers, vinegar, water, sea salt and honey.
2. Mix until all ingredients are well combined.

3. Transfer the mixture to a large glass jar or bottle with an airtight lid.
4. Place in a cool, dark place for at least 2 weeks, or up to 4 weeks.
5. When ready, strain the relish using a cheesecloth and discard peppers.
6. Transfer the relish to a clean jar with an airtight lid and store in the refrigerator.

Nutrition information: Calorie 172 | Fat 1g | Cholesterol 0mg | Sodium 4174mg | Carbohydrates 36g | Protein 2g.

68. Fermented marinated artichokes

Fermented Marinated Artichokes is a traditional Italian recipe which can make an amazing dish of artichoke hearts marinated in a flavorful mix of herbs and spices, plus a zesty fermented brine.
Serving: 8-10
Preparation Time: 15 minutes
Ready Time: 24 hours

Ingredients:
- 2 large jars artichoke hearts
- 2 cups white wine
- 1/2 cup salt
- 4 shallots, sliced
- 4 cloves garlic, crushed
- 1 tablespoon capers
- 1 tablespoon fresh rosemary, minced
- 1 tablespoon fresh thyme, minced
- 1 tablespoon fresh oregano, minced
- 1 teaspoon black peppercorns
- 2 bay leaves

Instructions:
1. Drain the artichoke hearts and transfer them to a large bowl.
2. Combine the white wine, salt, shallots, garlic, capers, rosemary, thyme, oregano, black peppercorns, and bay leaves in a saucepan over medium-high heat. Bring to a boil, stirring often.
3. Remove the brine from the heat and let cool to room temperature.
4. Pour the cooled brine over the artichoke hearts and stir to combine.

5. Cover the bowl and let the artichokes marinate in the refrigerator for 24 hours.
6. Transfer the marinated artichokes to a serving dish and serve.

Nutrition information: Per serving (based on 10 servings): Calories: 32, Fat: 0g, Carbohydrates: 4g, Protein: 0g, Sodium: 1012mg

69. Fermented sunchoke pickles

Fermented Sunchoke Pickles are a delicious and healthy way to enjoy sunchokes. With their crunchy texture and tart flavor, they make the perfect accompaniment to any meal.
Serving: 4 people
Preparation Time: 10 minutes
Ready Time: 5 days

Ingredients:
• 8 sunchokes, scrubbed and cut into ½ inch pieces
• 4 cups warm water
• 2 tablespoons salt
• 1 teaspoon sugar

Instructions:
1. In a large bowl, combine the warm water, salt, and sugar. Stir to dissolve.
2. Place the sunchoke pieces in the brine and make sure they are completely submerged.
3. Place a plate over the mixture and hold it in place with something heavy, like a jar filled with water. This will keep the sunchokes submerged in the brine.
4. Cover the bowl with a clean kitchen towel.
5. Let the mixture sit in a dark, cool place for 5 days, stirring every day.
6. After 5 days, the pickles are ready to eat or store in the refrigerator.

Nutrition information (per serving):
Calories: 44 kcal, Carbohydrates: 9 g, Protein: 1 g, Fat: 0 g, Sodium: 542 mg

70. Fermented pickled green tomatoes

Fermented pickled green tomatoes are a classic Mediterranean side dish. They are flavorful, tangy, and pickled with herbs and spices for an extra burst of flavor. This recipe is easy to make and is sure to be a crowd pleaser.

Serving: 4

Preparation time: 5 minutes

Ready time: 2 weeks

Ingredients:

- 2 lbs small green tomatoes
- 1/4 cup Himalayan salt
- 1 tbs pickling spice
- 2 tbs fresh herbs (oregano/thyme/parsley), finely chopped
- 2 cloves of garlic, chopped
- 2 cups filtered water
- 1/2 cup and apple cider vinegar

Instructions:

1. Wash the tomatoes and dry them. Slice each tomato into 4 slices and discard the stem end.
2. Put the tomatoes into a glass jar and add the Himalayan salt, pickling spice, fresh herbs, and garlic.
3. In a separate bowl, mix together the water and vinegar until combined.
4. Pour the liquid mixture over the tomatoes and seal the jar tightly.
5. Place the jar in a cool, dark place for 2 weeks to allow the tomatoes to ferment and pickle.

Nutrition information:

Serving size: 1/4 cup

Calories: 15 kcal

Total Fat: 0g

Saturated Fat: 0g

Trans Fat: 0g

Cholesterol: 0mg

Sodium: 350mg

Total Carbohydrates: 3.2g

Dietary Fiber: 0.7g
Sugars: 1.2g
Protein: 0.8g

71. Fermented cabbage and carrot salad

Fermented cabbage and carrot salad is a delicious and healthy dish to enjoy. It is a perfect accompaniment for any dish and will bring a lot of nutrition and flavor to your meal.
Serving: 6-8
Preparation time: 5 minutes
Ready time: 8-10 hours

Ingredients:
- 1 small head of green cabbage
- 1 large carrot
- 2 tablespoons salt
- 1/2 teaspoon sugar
- 1/2 teaspoon caraway seeds
- 2 cloves garlic, minced
- 2 tablespoons apple cider vinegar

Instructions:
1. Peel the carrot and grate it finely.
2. Shred the cabbage into thin strips and place them in a large bowl.
3. Add the grated carrot, salt, sugar, caraway, garlic, and apple cider vinegar.
4. Mix all Ingredients together and transfer to a Mason jar or glass container.
5. Let the mixture sit for 8-10 hours in a dark place at room temperature.
6. When the fermentation is done, transfer to the refrigerator and let it chill.
7. Serve chilled with your favorite dishes.

Nutrition information:
Calories: 83 kcal
Carbohydrates: 10 g
Protein: 2 g

Fat: 2 g
Saturated Fat: 1 g
Cholesterol: 0 mg
Sodium: 719 mg
Potassium: 384 mg
Fiber: 3 g
Sugar: 5 g
Vitamin A: 1981 IU
Vitamin C: 35 mg
Calcium: 49 mg
Iron: 1 mg

72. Fermented lemon garlic green beans

Fermented lemon garlic green beans is a flavorful and easy to make side dish. Its zesty flavor, crunchy texture, and probiotic health benefits make it a great pick for a delicious and healthy meal.
Serving: 4-6
Preparation time: 10 minutes
Ready time: 1-2 weeks

Ingredients:
- 2 tablespoons of Sea Salt
- 18 ounces of Green Beans
- 6 cloves of Garlic, peeled and crushed
- 1 medium Lemon, zested and juice
- 2 tablespoons of Unrefined Coconut Oil

Instructions:
1. In a medium sized bowl, mix together the sea salt, garlic, lemon juice, and coconut oil.
2. Once completely combined, pour the mixture over the green beans and mix to ensure all the green beans are completely coated.
3. Place the green beans in a jar, leaving 1-2 inches of headspace for the fermentation process.
4. Place the jar in a corner of your kitchen and leave for 1-2 weeks. Check the beans daily to ensure that the liquid is covering the beans.
5. After 1-2 weeks, the beans will be ready to enjoy!

Nutrition information (per serving):
Calories: 60
Total Fat: 2.5g
Saturated Fat: 1.5g
Carbohydrates: 8g
Protein: 2g
Fiber: 3g

73. Fermented ginger beet salad

This Fermented Ginger Beet Salad is a simple yet colorful dish packed with flavor and nutrition. Its unique combination of crunchy, sweet, and tangy Ingredients will delight your taste buds and boost your health. Servings: 4-6 Preparation Time: 15 minutes Ready Time: 2 hours

Ingredients:
5-6 medium beets, peeled and chopped into 1-inch cubes
3 cloves garlic, minced
1/4 cup olive oil
2 tablespoons of freshly grated ginger
1/4 cup of freshly squeezed lime juice
3-4 teaspoons of Himalayan pink salt

Instructions:
1. Preheat oven to 400°F.
2. Place the beets and garlic on a baking sheet. Drizzle with olive oil and sprinkle with ginger, lime juice, and salt.
3. Roast for 30-35 minutes or until beets are fork-tender.
4. Place the roasted beets in a glass jar and pour the remaining marinade from the baking sheet over the roasted vegetables.
5. Secure the lid and store in a cool place for at least 2 hours before serving.

Nutrition information:
Calories: 182
Fat: 11 g
Carbohydrates: 19 g

Protein: 2 g
Sugar: 9 g

74. Fermented pickled okra

Fermented pickled okra is a traditional Southern dish, featuring okra pickled in a brine of vinegar, celery seed, sugar and water and then left to ferment. The result is a tart, flavorful snack that's packed with probiotics, vitamins and minerals.
Serving: Makes 4 servings
Preparation time: 35 minutes
Ready time: 35 minutes

Ingredients:
- 2 pounds small okra
- 4 tablespoons celery seed
- 4 tablespoons sugar
- 2 cups distilled white vinegar
- 1 cup lukewarm water

Instructions:
1. Sterilize a 4-quart jar and lid with boiling water. Place the okra in the jar.
2. In a bowl, combine the celery seed, sugar, vinegar and water. Stir until the sugar is completely dissolved.
3. Pour the brine over the okra until it is completely submerged. Place the lid on the jar and set aside to ferment at room temperature for 3-4 days.
4. Once the okra is fermented to your liking, transfer to the refrigerator or another cool place. The pickles will last up to 3 weeks in the refrigerator.

Nutrition information
Per Serving: 90 Calories, 0g Fat, 20g Carbohydrates, 1g Protein, 0g Fiber

75. Fermented radish and cucumber salad

Fermented radish and cucumber salad is a tangy and flavorful side dish that is popular in Eastern Asian cuisine. It is full of healthy probiotics and delicious, savory flavors.
Serving: 4 servings
Preparation Time: 15 minutes
Ready Time: 8 - 12 hours

Ingredients:
- 6 small radishes, thinly sliced
- 1 cucumber, thinly sliced
- 1/4 cup white vinegar
- 3 cloves garlic, minced
- 2 scallions, thinly sliced
- 2 tablespoons of sesame oil
- 1 teaspoon of ground ginger
- Salt and pepper to taste

Instructions:
1. In a large bowl, combine the radishes and cucumbers.
2. In a small bowl or jar, whisk together the vinegar, garlic, salt, pepper, sesame oil, and ginger.
3. Pour the mixture over the radishes and cucumbers and mix everything together.
4. Cover the bowl and set aside at room temperature for 8-12 hours for the vegetables to ferment.
5. Once the vegetables are done fermenting, add the scallions and stir to combine.
6. Serve the salad cold or at room temperature.

Nutrition information:
Serving size: 1/4 of entire recipe
Calories: 82
Carbs: 14 g
Fat: 6 g
Protein: 1 g
Sodium: 42 mg

76. Fermented bell pepper hot sauce

Fermented bell pepper hot sauce is a fiery and flavorful sauce perfect for adding a touch of heat to tacos, burgers, sandwiches, and more.
Serving: Makes 4-6 servings
Preparation Time: 10 minutes
Ready Time: 1-2 weeks

Ingredients:
• 2 pounds bell peppers
• 2 tablespoons Kosher salt
• 2 tablespoons honey
• 2 tablespoons apple cider vinegar

Instructions:
1. Rinse and dry the peppers, then dice them into small cubes.
2. Place the diced peppers into an airtight, non-reactive container and add the salt, honey, and vinegar.
3. Mix everything together so that the peppers are evenly coated with the Ingredients.
4. Tightly lid the container and place in a warm, dark place for 1-2 weeks, periodically checking on the peppers and stirring them.
5. After 1-2 weeks, transfer the peppers and remaining liquid to a blender and blend until smooth.
6. Transfer the fermented bell pepper hot sauce to a sealed container and store in the refrigerator for up to 3 months.

Nutrition information: Estimated nutritional values per serving: Calories: 60, Fat: 0.07g, Sodium: 1,102mg, Carbohydrates: 15g, Protein: 2g

77. Fermented blueberry jam

Fermented blueberry jam is a delicious, sweet yet tart condiment that is made by preserving blueberries through fermentation. It can be used to top tasty toast, baguette, or dolloped on top of fresh yogurt.
Serving: makes 24 servings (2 tablespoons/serving)
Preparation Time: 10 minutes

Ready Time: 2 days

Ingredients:
• 4 cups organic blueberries
• 2 tablespoons water
• 2 tablespoons honey
• 2 tablespoons unrefined sea salt

Instructions:
1. Rinse the blueberries and place them in a bowl. Mash them slightly with a potato masher.
2. In a separate bowl, mix together the water, honey, and sea salt. Stir until combined.
3. Pour the mixture over the blueberries, and stir until the blueberries are completely coated.
4. Transfer the mixture to a clean glass jar, and seal it with the lid.
5. Place the jar in a warm, sunny spot for two days to help the fermentation process.
6. After two days, check to make sure the blueberries have fermented; they should be slightly puckered and have a mildly sour smell.
7. Once fermented, transfer the jam to the refrigerator. It should keep for up to two months.

Nutrition information: Per 2 tablespoon serving: 35 calories, 0 g fat, 9 g carbohydrates, 0 g protein, 2 g sugar.

78. Fermented mango chutney

Fermented mango chutney is a traditional Indian condiment, made with a mix of fragrant spices and tangy mango.
Serving: Makes 4 servings.
Preparation Time: 15 minutes
Ready Time: 1 hour

Ingredients:
- 2 large ripe mangoes, peeled and chopped
- 2 tablespoons olive oil
- 1 teaspoon sea salt

- 1 teaspoon cumin powder
- 1 teaspoon ground coriander
- 1 teaspoon ground ginger
- 2 cloves garlic, minced
- 1 teaspoon garam masala
- 1 teaspoon turmeric
- 1 teaspoon sugar
- ½ teaspoon chilli powder

Instructions:
1. Heat the olive oil in a medium saucepan over medium-high heat.
2. Add the mango, sea salt, cumin, coriander, ginger, garlic, garam masala, turmeric, sugar and chilli powder. Stir to combine.
3. Cook, stirring occasionally, for 8 minutes, or until everything is softened and fragrant.
4. Transfer the chutney mixture to a jar and allow to cool to room temperature.
5. Screw on the lid and leave to ferment in a dark place at room temperature for 8-24 hours.
6. Transfer the chutney to a bowl and enjoy as a condiment to liven up your eating experience.

Nutrition information: (Per serving):
Calories: 130
Protein: 1g
Fat: 9g
Carbohydrates: 12g
Fiber: 4g
Sugar: 6g
Sodium: 350mg

79. Fermented pineapple salsa

Fermented Pineapple Salsa is a flavorful twist on traditional salsa recipes. It has a tangy, sweet and spicy flavor that will tantalize your taste buds! This recipe is easy to make and sure to be a hit.
Serving: Makes 4 servings
Prep Time: 10 minutes

Ready Time: 24 hours to ferment

Ingredients:
- 1/2 pineapple, diced
- 1/4 cup diced red bell pepper
- 1/4 cup diced green bell pepper
- 1/4 cup sliced red onion
- 1 diced jalapeño
- 1/4 cup chopped cilantro
- Juice of 1 lime
- 1/2 teaspoon sea salt
- 1/4 teaspoon ground black pepper
- 2 cloves garlic, minced

Instructions:
1. In a large bowl, combine pineapple, bell peppers, red onion, jalapeño, cilantro, lime juice, salt, pepper and garlic.
2. Place the salsa in a mason jar and seal tightly. Stir it a few times over the course of the day to mix it up.
3. Place the lid on the salsa and let it ferment at room temperature for 24 hours.
4. After 24 hours, taste the salsa and adjust seasoning if desired.
5. Transfer to an airtight container and place in the refrigerator to store.

Nutrition information (per serving):
Calories: 65, Total fat: 0.5 g, Saturated fat: 0.1 g, Cholesterol: 0 mg, Sodium: 220 mg, Total carbohydrate: 16 g, Dietary fiber: 3 g, Protein: 1 g.

80. Fermented apricot preserves

Fermented apricot preserves are a delicious and unique take on apricot preserves. The distinctive and flavorful preserves are made from fresh apricots and are an excellent accompaniment to various desserts and dishes.
Serving: 3-4
Preparation time: 10 minutes
Ready time: 1 hour

Ingredients:
- 1 lb fresh apricots
- 2 Tbsp honey
- 1 tsp lemon juice
- 1 cup plain yogurt
- 2 Tbs honey
- 1/2 Tbs sea salt

Instructions:
1. Start by washing and drying the apricots. Cut them in half and discard the pits.
2. Place the apricots in a large bowl and add the lemon juice, honey, yogurt, and sea salt. Mix all Ingredients together to evenly coat the apricots.
3. Put the mixture in a jar and place it in a cool, dark place. Allow it to ferment for around 1 hour.
4. Once the preserves have fermented, blend the mixture in a food processor until it is smooth.
5. Serve the preserves with your favorite desserts or dishes.

Nutrition information: Calories: 35, Fat: 0 g, Carbohydrates: 8 g, Protein: 1 g, Fiber: 1 g

81. Fermented strawberry rhubarb compote

Fermented strawberry rhubarb compote is a delicious side dish that brings together a delightful combination of fruity flavours.
Serving: 4
Preparation Time: 10 minutes
Ready Time: 2 to 3 days

Ingredients:
- 2 cups fresh strawberries, diced
- 2 cups diced rhubarb
- 3 tablespoons sugar
- 2 teaspoons active dry yeast
- 2 tablespoons water

Instructions:

1. In a medium saucepan, combine the strawberries, rhubarb, and sugar. Cook over medium heat, stirring until the fruit is soft and the mixture starts to thicken, about 10 minutes.
2. In a small bowl, combine the yeast and water and stir until the yeast is dissolved.
3. Add the yeast mixture to the fruit mixture and stir until combined.
4. Transfer the compote to a clean glass jar and cover tightly. Set aside at room temperature for 2 to 3 days, stirring every day.
5. Serve the compote over ice cream, oatmeal, yogurt, toast, or anything else you can think of!

Nutrition information: (Per Serving)

Calories: 72 kcal
Total Fat: 0 g
Saturated Fat: 0 g
Cholesterol: 0 mg
Sodium: 1 mg
Carbohydrates: 18 g
Fiber: 2 g
Sugar: 12 g
Protein: 1 g

82. Fermented peach butter

Fermented peach butter is a scrumptious close-textured spread that uses natural fermentation processes to enhance the flavor of the peaches. It can be used for spreading on breads and toast or added to sauces, yogurts, and smoothies.

Serving: Makes about 2 cups
Preparation Time: 15 minutes
Ready Time: 3 to 6 days

Ingredients:

- 4-5 firm, ripened peaches
- A quarter teaspoon of salt
- 2 tablespoons of raw honey

Instructions:

1. Peel, pit, and chop the peaches into small cubes.
2. Place the cubes into a large, clean jar and add the salt and honey.
3. Stir all the Ingredients together until well blended.
4. Seal the jar and leave it on the counter in a warm area for 3-6 days.
5. Stir the mixture once a day with a clean wooden spoon.
6. Once the mixture has thickened to a spreadable consistency, blend it until smooth using a food processor or blender.
7. Store in an airtight container in the fridge.

Nutrition information: Serving size 2 tablespoons; Calories 42; Fat 0g; Sodium 32mg; Carbohydrates 10g; Protein 0.4g; Sugars 6.4g

83. Fermented raspberry vinegar

Fermented raspberry vinegar is a condiment made with raspberries that have been fermented over a period of time. It has a tart and slightly sweet taste, adding great flavor to a variety of dishes.
Serving: 4-6
Preparation time: 10 minutes
Ready time: 2-3 weeks

Ingredients:

- 2 cups fresh raspberries
- 1 cup water
- 2-3 tablespoons white sugar
- 1/4 cup apple cider vinegar

Instructions:

1. In a medium saucepan, bring 2 cups of raspberries and 1 cup of water to a boil. Simmer for 5 minutes, stirring occasionally.
2. Strain the raspberry liquid through a fine-mesh sieve. Set aside.
3. In a separate bowl, add 2-3 tablespoons of sugar to the strained raspberry liquid and mix until fully dissolved.
4. Pour the mixture into a jar or container, and add 1/4 cup of apple cider vinegar. Stir it together to combine.

5. Place the container in a cool, dark place and cover with a cheesecloth. Allow it to ferment for 2-3 weeks, stirring with a sterilized spoon every few days.
6. Once the fermented raspberry vinegar is done, strain it through a fine-mesh sieve to remove any solids.
7. Store the vinegar in a clean, air-tight container in the refrigerator.

Nutrition information: Per Serving: Serving Size: 2 tablespoons Calories: 20 Total Fat: 0g Cholesterol: 0mg Sodium: 2mg Total Carbohydrates: 5g Dietary Fiber: 0g Sugars: 4g Protein: 0g

84. Fermented blackberry syrup

Rich and tangy fermented blackberry syrup is both delicious and easy to make. This syrup is a perfect topping for pancakes, waffles, ice cream sundaes, muffins, and more.
Serving: Makes 4 cups
Preparation Time: 10 minutes
Ready Time: Overnight fermentation

Ingredients:
- 6 cups fresh blackberries
- 1 cup raw cane sugar
- 2 tablespoons raw apple cider vinegar

Instructions:
1. In a medium saucepan, combine the blackberries and sugar over medium heat.
2. Cook for about 8 minutes, stirring frequently, until the blackberries have softened and released their juice.
3. Allow the mixture to cool for 5 minutes.
4. Place the mixture into a glass jar or bowl and add the apple cider vinegar. Stir until completely combined.
5. Cover the jar with a tight-fitting lid or a piece of cheesecloth secured with an elastic band.
6. Place the jar in a cool, dark place and let it ferment overnight.
7. Strain the mixture through a fine-mesh sieve into a medium saucepan.
8. Heat the mixture over medium heat until it boils.

9. Reduce the heat and simmer for 10 minutes, stirring occasionally.
10. Remove the syrup from the heat and allow it to cool to room temperature.
11. Pour the syrup into a jar, seal it tightly, and store it in the fridge.

Nutrition information: Per 1/4 cup serving: 140 calories, 0g fat, 16g carbohydrate, 1g fiber, 11g sugar, and 0g protein.

85. Fermented apple cider vinegar

Fermented apple cider vinegar is acidic and full of flavor and a great addition to any meal. It is comparable to balsamic, although it is much sweeter in taste and pairs well with salads, fresh fruits, and grilled meats.
Serving: 1-2 tablespoons
Preparation Time: 5 minutes
Ready Time: 5 minutes

Ingredients:
- Fresh apples, quartered
- Unfiltered apple cider vinegar
- Filtered water

Instructions:
1. Place the quartered apples into a large jar.
2. Pour in the apple cider vinegar.
3. Fill the rest of the jar up with filtered water.
4. Close the jar tightly and let it sit in a cool, dark place for 2 weeks.
5. After two weeks, strain the mixture through a cheesecloth and store the liquid in a bottle or glass jar.
6. Enjoy!

Nutrition information: Per serving: Calories: 5, Fat: 0g, Sodium: 0mg, Carbohydrates: 1g, Protein: 0g

86. Fermented pear and ginger relish

Fermented pear and ginger relish is a unique and special condiment with a zesty flavor and delightfully potent aroma. It is the perfect topping for practically any savory dish, and even pairs excellently with dessert.
Serving: 4-6
Preparation Time: 15 minutes
Ready Time: 2 weeks

Ingredients:
- 6 pears, chopped
- 1/4 cup fresh ginger, minced
- 2 cloves garlic, minced
- 2 tablespoons unrefined sea salt
- 1/4 teaspoon chili flakes
- 1/4 teaspoon tsp ground black pepper
- 2 tablespoons white sugar
- 2 bay leaves
- 4-6 500ml glass jars with lids

Instructions:
1. In a large bowl, combine the chopped pears, ginger, garlic, salt, chili flakes, pepper, and sugar. Mix until all ingredients are fully combined.
2. Fill each glass jar to the brim with the pear and ginger mixture.
3. Add 1 bay leaf to each jar. Close each jar tightly with a lid.
4. Store the jars in a dark place at room temperature for 2 weeks, being sure to give each jar a gentle swirl once a day to mix up the fermenting ingredients.
5. After 2 weeks, your relish is ready to enjoy!

Nutrition information: (per serving):
Calorie: 50 kcal,
Fat: 0 g,
Saturated Fat: 0 g,
Cholesterol: 0 mg,
Sodium: 250 mg,
Carbohydrate: 13 g,
Fiber: 2 g,
Sugar: 8 g,
Protein: 0 g.

87. Fermented cranberry orange sauce

This vibrant and zesty Fermented Cranberry Orange Sauce is the perfect topping for savory pancakes, roasted turkey, and more! It takes just minutes to stir together and is sure to become a favorite in your holiday spread.
Serving: Serves 8
Preparation Time: 10 minutes
Ready Time: 2 days

Ingredients:
- 2 cups freshly squeezed orange juice
- ½ cup honey
- 2 tablespoons apple cider vinegar
- 2 tablespoons freshly grated ginger
- ¼ teaspoon sea salt

Instructions:
1. In a bowl, combine the orange juice, honey, apple cider vinegar, ginger, and sea salt. Stir until fully combined. Place the mixture into a quart-sized mason jar.
2. Cover the jar with the lid and a cloth napkin and secure with a rubber band. Place the jar in a cool, dark space.
3. Allow the ferments to sit for a minimum of 48 hours or until bubbles start to form in the jar. Refrigerate for up to 3 weeks.
4. Enjoy as topping on pancakes, roasted turkey, or your favorite dish!

Nutrition information:
- Calories: 145
- Fat: 0g
- Cholesterol: 0mg
- Sodium: 112mg
- Carbohydrates: 36g
- Fiber: 1g
- Sugar: 34g
- Protein: 1g

88. Fermented elderflower cordial

Fermented elderflower cordial is a unique and fresh-tasting concoction made from elderflowers, lemons, and honey. Full of fragrant floral notes, it makes for a great summer drink or flavor addition to many dishes.
Serving: Makes 2 quarts / 2 liters
Preparation time: 45 minutes
Ready time: 4 days

Ingredients:
- 20 elderflower heads
- 10 lemons
- 2 quarts / 2 liters boiling water
- 2 lb / 1 kg superfine sugar
- 1 oz / 30 g fresh ginger root
- 2 heaped tablespoons of champagne or white wine yeast
- 2 lemons, juiced
- 1 lb / 500g honey

Instructions:
1. Place the elderflower heads and lemons in a large heatproof bowl.
2. Mix the boiling water with the sugar and stir until sugar dissolves.
3. Pour over elderflower heads and lemons making sure they are all covered.
4. Cover the bowl and allow to ferment for 4 days.
5. Peel and grate the ginger root and add it to the mixture along with the yeast.
6. Squeeze the 2 lemons and stir the juice into the mixture.
7. Add the honey and stir until it is dissolved in the cordial.
8. Strain the cordial through a muslin cloth, squeezing out as much of the liquid as possible.
9. Transfer the fermented cordial into bottles and seal them.

Nutrition information: Per 100 ml:
- Calories: 110 kcal
- Protein: 0 g
- Total fat: 0 g
- Total carbohydrates: 26 g
- Sodium: 5 mg
- Sugar: 21 g

89. Fermented grape jelly

Fermented grape jelly is a unique, delightfully-sweet, and easy-to-make jelly that uses freshly-pressed grape juice and simple ingredients.
Serving: Makes 2 quarts
Preparation Time: 25 minutes
Ready Time: 1-2 weeks

Ingredients:

- 8 cups freshly pressed grape juice
- 1 teaspoon bread yeast
- 2 tablespoons of white sugar
- ½ teaspoon citric acid
- ½ teaspoon of sea salt

Instructions:

1. In a large pot, combine the grape juice and yeast. Stir to combine, then turn the heat on low and simmer for about 10 minutes, stirring occasionally.
2. Add the sugar, citric acid, and salt and stir to combine. Turn off the heat.
3. Divide the jelly between two jars, filling each jar up to the brim. Cover each jar with a kitchen towel or cheesecloth and set aside in a cool, dark place to ferment.
4. Let the jelly ferment for 1-2 weeks, stirring every few days. Once the jelly has reached your desired flavor, store in the refrigerator for up to 3 months.

Nutrition information:

Calories: 110, Fat: 0g, Carbohydrate: 26g, Sugar: 16g, Protein: 0g, Sodium: 61mg

90. Fermented pomegranate molasses

Fermented pomegranate molasses is a rich and tangy condiment made with pomegranate juice, sugar, and salt. It adds a tart and sweet flavor to foods such as salads, sandwiches, and even grilled meats.
Serving: 3-4
Preparation Time: 20 minutes
Ready Time: 4 hours

Ingredients:
- 1 liter of pomegranate juice
- 1/3 cup of sugar
- 1 teaspoon of salt

Instructions:
1. In a medium-sized bowl, combine pomegranate juice, sugar and salt until the mixture is dissolved.
2. Place the mixture into a large jar and cover with a lid.
3. Store the jar in a cool, dark place for at least four hours, or overnight.
4. Uncover the jar and strain the contents into a separate bowl.
5. Let the mixture cool for at least an hour.
6. Pour the cooled mixture into a sterilized jar and store in the refrigerator until ready to use.

Nutrition information:
One tablespoon of Fermented Pomegranate Molasses contains approximately 22 calories, 0.4 grams of fat, 5.4 grams of carbohydrates, and 0.5 grams of protein.

91. Fermented lemon curd

Sweet yet tangy, Fermented Lemon Curd is a delicious tart condiment that can be used to top a variety of dishes. Its combination of yogurt and lemon juice is creamy, flavorful, and fun to make.
Serving: 8
Preparation time: 10 minutes
Ready time: 4 hours

Ingredients:
• 2 cups plain yogurt

• 2 large lemons, zested and juiced
• 1/3 cup honey

Instructions:
1. In a medium bowl, whisk together yogurt, lemon juice, and honey.
2. Cover the bowl and place into refrigerator to ferment for 4 hours.
3. Once fermented, remove from refrigerator and stir in the zest from the lemons.
4. Spread the curd over your desired dish and enjoy!

Nutrition information: Serving size: 2 tablespoons. Calories: 73, Fat: 1.2g, Carbohydrates: 13.2g, Protein: 2.2g, Sodium: 21.2mg

92. Fermented cherry pie filling

Fermented cherry pie filling is a delicious and tart twist on a classic dessert. It features tart cherries that have been fermented with sugar and a splash of vinegar to enhance the flavor of the cherries.
Serving: 10
Preparation Time: 10 minutes
Ready Time: 2 hours 20 minutes

Ingredients:
- 3 cups fresh cherries
- 4 tablespoons sugar
- 2 tablespoons white vinegar
- 2 tablespoons cornstarch

Instructions:
1. Pit the cherries and place 1 cup of them in a bowl.
2. Add 1 tablespoon of sugar and 1 tablespoon of white vinegar to the cherry mixture.
3. Stir to combine and let the cherries sit for 2 hours.
4. Add the remaining 2 tablespoons of sugar, 1 tablespoon of white vinegar and 2 tablespoons of cornstarch to the cherry mixture.
5. Stir to combine until all the sugar is dissolved and all the liquid is absorbed.
6. Place the cherry mixture in a prepared pie crust.

7. Bake the pie in a 375°F oven for 30 minutes or until the crust is golden brown and the filling is thick and bubbly.

Nutrition information:
Serving Size 1/10th of recipe
Calories: 85 calories
Fat: 0.5 grams
Carbohydrates: 20 grams
Protein: 1 gram

93. Fermented fig and walnut spread

Fermented fig and walnut spread is a delicious and unique condiment that adds wonderful flavor to sandwiches, toast, bagels and crackers.
Serving: Makes about 2 cups
Preparation Time: 10 minutes
Ready Time: 8 days

Ingredients:
- 10 fresh figs, diced
- 1/4 cup white wine vinegar
- 1/4 cup chopped walnuts
- 1 teaspoon sea salt
- 1 teaspoon ground coriander

Instructions:
1. Place the diced figs in a medium bowl.
2. Add the vinegar, walnuts, salt and coriander, and mix to combine.
3. Transfer the mixture to a glass jar and seal tightly.
4. Place the jar in a cool, dark place for 8 days, shaking the jar every day or two.
5. After 8 days, remove the jar from its hiding place and open it. Give it a good stirring. The mixture will have a thick, spreadable consistency.
6. Store the fermented fig and walnut spread in a jar in the refrigerator for up to 2 weeks.

Nutrition information: Serving size 2 tablespoons; Calories 97; Fat 5g; Saturated Fat 1g; Cholesterol 0mg; Sodium 120mg; Carbohydrates 13g; Fiber 4g; Sugar 7g; Protein 2g.

94. Fermented plum sauce

Fermented plum sauce is a plum-based condiment that is popular as a topping and dipping sauce. It has a unique flavor that is both sweet and tart. It's easy to make and doesn't take much time, so give it a try!
Serving: 4
Preparation time: 10 minutes
Ready time: 1 hour

Ingredients:
- 11 ounces pitted plums
- 1/4 cup white vinegar
- 1 tablespoon white sugar
- 1/2 teaspoon sea salt
- 1 clove garlic, minced

Instructions:
1. In a small saucepan, heat the plums, vinegar, sugar, salt, and garlic over low heat for about 10 minutes, stirring occasionally.
2. Let the mixture cool completely, and then transfer to a clean glass jar with a lid.
3. Cover the jar with tinfoil, and keep it at room temperature for 1 hour.
4. Once the fermentation process is finished, refrigerate the sauce for up to one month.

Nutrition information: 35 calories, 0.6 grams fat, 8 grams carbohydrates, 0.4 grams protein.

95. Fermented honey garlic glaze

Introducing the delicious Fermented Honey Garlic Glaze! This recipe is a savory, sweet, and pungent condiment with an underlying umami that can turn any dish into an extraordinary culinary masterpiece.

Serving: This recipe serves 8 people.
Preparation time: Total preparation time is 8 hours.
Ready time: Total ready time is 24 hours.

Ingredients:
- 2 pounds freshly peeled garlic
- 2 cups honey
- 1 cup red miso paste
- ½ cup distilled white vinegar
- 1 teaspoon red pepper flakes

Instructions:
1. Place the peeled garlic cloves in a wide-mouth glass jar and add enough of the distilled white vinegar so that the garlic is fully submerged.
2. Cover the jar with a lid and leave to ferment for 8 hours in a cool, dark place.
3. After 8 hours, drain the garlic cloves and discard the vinegar.
4. Place the garlic cloves in a blender or food processor, along with the honey, miso paste, and red pepper flakes.
5. Process the mixture until a thick glaze is formed.
6. Transfer the glaze to a storing container, cover with a lid or plastic wrap, and let it ferment at room temperature for another 16 hours.
7. Once ready, the Fermented Honey Garlic Glaze can be served as a condiment or spread on breads or burgers.

Nutrition information:
Serving size: 2 tablespoons (30g)
Calories: 135
Total Fat: 0.3g
Saturated Fat: 0.2g
Unsaturated Fat: 0.1g
Trans Fat: 0g
Cholesterol: 0mg
Total Carbohydrates: 33.7g
Dietary Fiber: 6.2g
Sugars: 25.5g
Protein: 3.2g

CONCLUSION

Cookbook "Step-by-Step Fermentation: 95 Beginner-Friendly Recipes for Fermenting Foods"

In conclusion, the cookbook "Step-by-Step Fermentation: 95 Beginner-Friendly Recipes for Fermenting Foods" is an invaluable and comprehensive resource for those looking to embark on the journey of creating flavorful and nutritious fermented foods in the comfort of their own home. This user-friendly cookbook provides a thorough overview of the fermentation process, containing clear instructions and plenty of helpful information on the organisms responsible, the necessary tools and ingredients, and the traditional recipes involved. Furthermore, it features an abundance of recipes ranging from the basic to the unique, ensuring that you can easily find the dish best suited to your taste and level of culinary expertise. With this cookbook, you too can try your hand at creating a wide array of flavourful and healthy fermented food products and join the age-old tradition of fermentation. So, start fermenting today to enjoy the flavours and health benefits of fermented foods for years to come!

www.ingramcontent.com/pod-product-compliance
Ingram Content Group UK Ltd.
Pitfield, Milton Keynes, MK11 3LW, UK
UKHW022014190726
13853UKWH00005B/1933

9 798857 593424